MAKING
Wirecraft
CARDS

MAKING
Wirecraft
CARDS

Kate MacFadyen

GUILD OF MASTER CRAFTSMAN PUBLICATIONS

First published 2004 by
Guild of Master Craftsman Publications Ltd
Castle Place, 166 High Street,
Lewes, East Sussex BN7 1XU

Reprinted 2005

ISBN 1 86108 393 9

A catalogue record for this book is available from the British Library.

Production Manager: Hilary MacCallum
Managing Editor: Gerrie Purcell
Project Editor: Dominique Page
Book Design: Danny McBride
Cover Design: GMC Studio

Set in Swiss, Eurostyle Futura

Colour origination by Icon Reprographics
Printed and bound by Kyodo, Singapore

Measurements notice

Imperial measurements are conversions from metric; they have been rounded up or down
to the nearest ¼, ½ or whole inch. When following the projects, use either the metric or the
imperial measurements; do not mix units.

I would like to dedicate this book to my mother,
Jean Edgington, my mentor and friend, to thank her for all
her support and encouragement over the years.

Contents

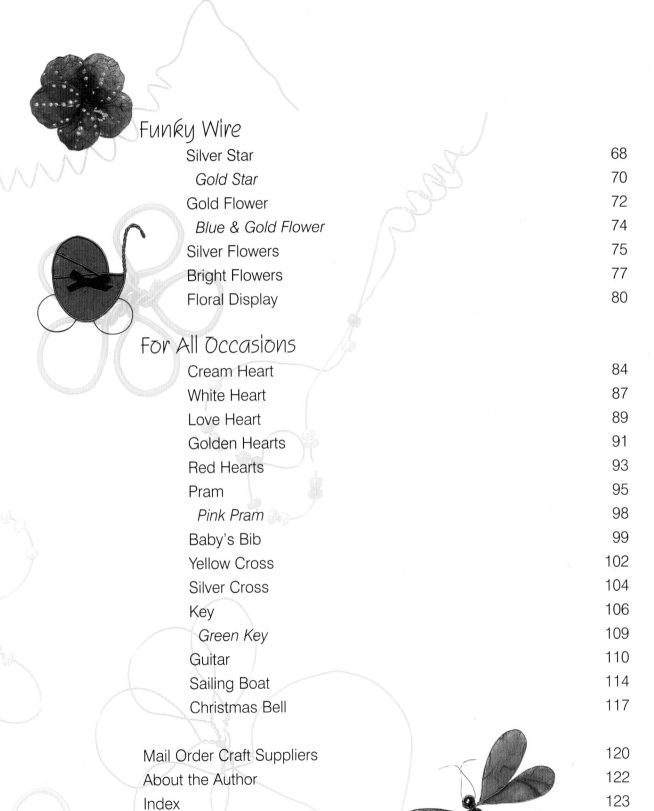

Funky Wire

For All Occasions

A few years ago I was introduced to wirecraft. The class that I attended made a dragonfly, a butterfly and a very simple flower. I thoroughly enjoyed the class and loved how easily you could transform the wire into beautiful shapes.

Having spent hours at home making dragonflies for gift cards, I thought I would see if I could improve on them by adding colour. I had bought lots of mulberry paper to use as backing for my cards, and had laid a dragonfly on the paper. It looked so pretty that I began to experiment with glues to see if I could stick the paper to the wire. I discovered I could, and was so pleased with the result that I tried it with a butterfly and then a variety of flowers.

Over the last two years I have designed all the projects in this book, but I am sure there are many more that could be created, so once you have learned the basic technique, the sky really is the limit. Wirecraft can also be put to many uses, not just decorating cards – try decorating gift boxes, candles or table name-settings.

Have fun!

Kate

Getting Started

Wirecraft is not difficult to master but there are a few things you need to know before you get started. There are certain materials and equipment that you will require, and you will find information on these in the first part of this chapter. If you are new to card-making there are step-by-step instructions on how to make a basic card, plus there is a list of useful hints that should help you to avoid any mistakes.

Materials & Equipment

So much craft equipment and materials are available today, including decorative scissors, handmade papers, embossing tools, ribbons, punches, rubber stamps, peel-off greetings, and many other striking ready-made embellishments, that the options open to you and the variety of cards that you can make is simply enormous. Here you will find all you need to know about the basic materials and equipment you will require, plus a list of additional items that will prove useful for individual projects.

Essential items

Cards

The basic card size is a C.6, which is 6 x 4in (15 x 10cm) when folded and will fit most ready-made envelopes sold in stationers. You can buy them from craft shops and mail order companies in gold, silver, plus a multitude of other colours (see pages 120–121 for mail order addresses). Thicker, textured card will guarantee a high-quality card, while thinner card is acceptable but tends to bend more. It is useful, however, for layering the front of a card, for rubber stamping, or for punching with decorative punches.

Wires

The wires come in a range of widths (gauges) and colours. Usually, the higher the gauge number the thinner the wire. For flower centres and delicate work I use 34-gauge and for flower petals and stems I use 28-gauge.

Often, I will match the wire colour to the colour of paper I intend to use, but if you do not wish to buy lots of different colours then I suggest you buy one reel of gold and one of silver in 28-gauge and 34-gauge. Having tried and tested a wide range of wires, I have decided that the copper-based wires are the best, as they are so supple and therefore easy to manipulate. Unfortunately, though, gold and silver wires tend not to be copper-based.

For some of the projects I have used textured wires that are coated with threads. These are thicker and heavier but nonetheless very easy to mould into interesting shapes. If you cannot find textured wires, though, 24-gauge wires are a suitable alternative.

Papers

I mainly use mulberry papers, which come in a wonderful array of colours. They stick quickly and easily to the glued wires, and as they are so thin and pliable it is easy to trim the excess paper away. I have, on occasions, used tissue papers, but have found that they tend to warp when wet and the colours can run. On some of the projects, such as the Pram and Baby's Bib (see pages 95–98 and 99–101), I have used thicker handmade papers which are also easy to use. I sometimes use webbing ribbon as an alternative to paper. This is a very fine, almost gauze-like material, which looks incredibly delicate but is not at all difficult to work with.

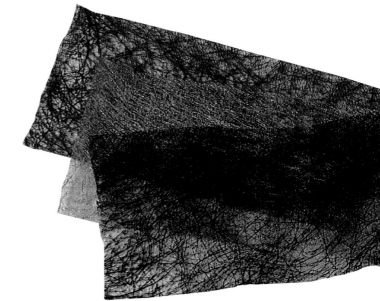

Beads

You will find that there are lots of different sizes and colours of beads available. For the flower centres I prefer to use embroidery beads as they are small and can give the impression of pollen, but I also use seed beads and larger beads that you can buy in small packs. Occasionally I will even raid old necklaces that I've bought at jumble sales and charity shops. Old necklaces are so cheap and the beads are very attractive.

Glue

I have experimented with many types of glue but the one that works the best in my opinion is an all-purpose glue for metals and plastics that is 'stringy' in texture and comes in a tube. White PVA and PPA glue are not suitable, as they are wet and don't adhere to the metal frame (it is the 'stringy' part of the glue that you need to attach to the wire). I have tried gel glues, and although they can work, they come out of the tubes in quite large lumps which are then difficult to smooth onto thin wire.

Buy the smallest tube you can find because you will want a small nozzle. Some time ago I bought a very large tube thinking it would last for ages but not only did it thicken with age, it poured out of the tube the moment I unscrewed the lid.

Glue dots are also invaluable for attaching decorations that are particularly small.

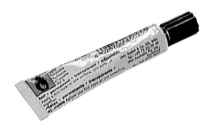

Scissors

You will need a variety of scissors. I have found that the wires are thin enough not to require wire-cutters – an old pair of scissors that you don't mind blunting will be sufficient. Small curved nail scissors or craft scissors are necessary for trimming the paper close to the wire (a curved blade enables you to closely follow the shape of the wire). You will also need a general-purpose pair for cutting the mulberry paper. Finally, a deckle-edged pair of scissors is a good investment for card-making, as you can quickly and easily create an attractive effect with them.

Other Useful Items

Ribbons and bows

Backing papers

Webbing ribbon (also known as angel hair)

Foam pads

Diamond dots

Double-sided tape

Paper towels

Scalpel or craft knife

Metal safety ruler

Self-healing cutting mat

Glue sticks

Rubber stamps

Ink pads

Decorative punches

Cocktail stick or cotton bud (without the cotton wool) for shaping flower stems

A lightbox and embossing tool for framing or adding additional embellishements to cards

Felt-tipped pens

Pastel chalks

Card-Making

If you are new to card-making, read through the instructions below and have a go at making this simple card.

1. Cut a plain piece of white card measuring 8 x 6in (21 x 15cm).

2. Using an embossing tool and ruler, score a line that is 4in (10.5cm) from either end, then fold.

3. Cut a piece of red patterned backing paper measuring 5½ x 4in (14.5 x 10cm) then trim with deckle-edged scissors. Glue the back of the paper with a glue stick or double-sided tape and attach to the front of the white card.

4. Cut red pearlized card measuring 4¼ x 2¾in (11 x 7cm) and glue to the centre of your card.

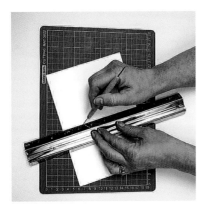

2

3

4

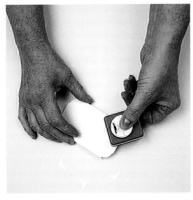

5

5. Cut a piece of white card measuring 4 x 2½in (10.5 x 6.5cm). Decorate the corners using a corner punch or decorative scissors. Glue to the centre of the red card.

6. Your card is now ready for your chosen embellishment.

6

Helpful Hints

1. Wire has a tendency to bend and knot when and where you don't want it to, and it tangles easily, especially if you cut a length too long. Between each loop that is formed I always gently run the length of wire between my finger and thumb. This will undo any kinks and keep the wire running smoothly.

2. I have stipulated a certain length of wire for each project and the size of the circle or loop that you will need to form. If you make the loop larger than stipulated you will not have enough wire to finish the flower. However, further wire can be added, and this is explained on page 23.

3. It can be difficult to find 34-gauge wire in the colours that are stated in some of the projects. If you cannot get hold of the coloured 34-gauge then it can be subsituted with either gold or silver, both of which are readily available.

4. Good light is important, as many of the wires are thin and light in colour, making them hard to see. Natural light is best but if you haven't got access to a window, a desk lamp is an effective alternative.

5. If you make a mistake when gluing paper to the wire frame or cut the paper too small, gently remove it then with a little nail polish remover and cotton wool, remove the glue from the wire frame so that you can start again.

6. Dried glue tends to show up on dark mulberry papers, especially red and purple, so use as little glue as possible or substitute them for a paler shade.

7. Mulberry paper has many uses for card-making. Not only can it be used to make petals for flowers, it can be wet-torn into many shapes (this technique is described on page 44). It is also very pretty as a backing layer to cards.

8. Always use a self-healing cutting mat when you're cutting card and paper with a craft knife. A wooden board will not only blunt your blade but the wood will grip it and make it difficult to control the cut.

9. Read each project thoroughly before you begin!

Wire Flowers

There are ten flower designs in this chapter but I suggest you start with the first: the Basic Flower. You may need to practise this many times before you are happy with your creation. The designs increase in difficulty but they are all made in the same way, by moulding wire loops and circles into petals and threading beads into the centre of the flower. To finish, they each have mulberry paper attached to the wire frames to imitate petals.

Basic Flower

Let your imagination run riot with this first project. The instructions below detail the wire, beads and paper I used to make the yellow flower pictured, but you could choose any coloured wire, mulberry paper and beads. By altering the colours you can create completely different looks. You could also try making the loops different sizes to create larger and smaller petals.

Basic Flower

The instructions:

1. Cut 18in (45cm) of 28-gauge gold wire. Find the centre of the wire and then form a loop with a 1¼in (3cm) diameter by crossing the wire over itself. Hold the join between your finger and thumb (I am right-handed, so I hold the wire in my left hand). As close to the join as possible, twist the loop three times with your other finger and thumb. You should have now completed one loop.

2. Working with either the right or left wire, make a second petal as close to the first as possible.

3. Continue to use the wire from the left and/or right until you have made five petals. There should be two pieces of wire left over. Take these two pieces to the back and twist together to form the stem. If you have made only four petals because you have run out of wire, don't worry, you've probably made them too big – this will have to be a four-petal flower!

4. Cut 6in (15cm) of 34-gauge gold wire. Wrap one end of the wire around the stem to fix into place.

5. Bring the long end of the wire up between two petals to the top of the flower.

6. Thread three yellow embroidery or seed beads onto the wire. Take the wire over the centre (the beads should sit in the centre of the flower) and down between two opposite petals and then up to the top again. Thread three more beads and repeat the process until you have approximately 12 beads in the centre (I'm afraid this is fiddly, as the beads keep falling down to the underneath of the flower but do persevere).

7. Spend a little time shaping the individual petals to a pleasing shape. It must be done now, as once the mulberry paper is attached it is too late.

You will need:

Wirecraft
18in (45cm) 28-gauge gold wire

6in (15cm) 34-gauge gold wire

Approx. 12 yellow embroidery/seed beads

Yellow mulberry paper

Cocktail stick/cotton bud

Kitchen paper

Glue

Shaped scissors

Card
8½ x 8¼in (22 x 21cm) white card

8 x 4in (20 x 10cm) patterned parchment paper

Double-sided tape

Glue dots

Diamond dot

1

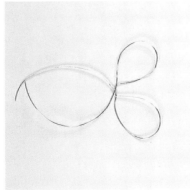

2

3

(See Tip on left.)

8. Cut four or five rectangular pieces of mulberry paper (depending on how many petals you have made). Make sure that each piece of paper is larger than the petals. (See Tip on left.)

9. Turn the flower over so the back of it is facing you and have a small piece of kitchen paper to hand. Carefully apply a very thin strip of glue around one petal then immediately use the kitchen paper to remove the excess glue.

10. Quickly place one of the cut pieces of paper to the underside of the petal frame, pressing gently between your fingers and thumb.

11. Turn the flower over to the front, and with your shaped scissors trim away the excess paper as close to the wire frame as possible. Continue in the same way, completing one petal at a time.

12. There are two ways you can complete the flowers stems:

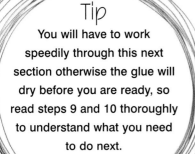

Tip

You will have to work speedily through this next section otherwise the glue will dry before you are ready, so read steps 9 and 10 thoroughly to understand what you need to do next.

4

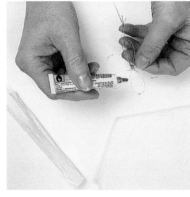

5

6

8

9

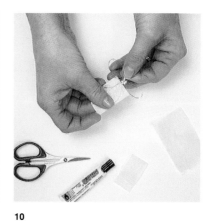

10

a. Cut off the shortest wire (1) and wrap the remainder around a cocktail stick or cotton bud to make a spring-like stem (2). If neither of the wire pieces are long enough you will need to add an extra length (see below).

or

b. Leave the wire straight and thread beads onto the entire length of the wire, securing the end by threading it through the last bead a second time. Cut off the excess wire.

Adding Wire

Take hold of the stem in one hand and wrap a new piece of wire around the stem, working up towards the flower and down again. This will secure the new wire to the stem, enabling you to cut off the wire that is too short.

To make the card:

1. Score and fold in half a piece of white card measuring 8½ x 8¼in (22 x 21cm).

2. Cut patterned parchment paper measuring 8 x 4in (20 x 10cm) and attach with small pieces of double-sided tape to the four corners.

3. Attach the flower with a glue dot.

4. Secure the stem with a glue dot.

5. Add a diamond dot at the base of the stem for decoration.

11

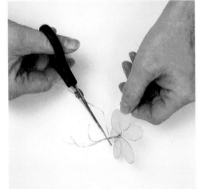

12a(1)

12a(2)

12b

Pink Clematis

Hopefully you will have now mastered the basic flower and are ready to move on to this pink clematis. The technique for each flower is the same, but the size and shape of the petal determines the flower. The clematis comes in a vast array of colours and sizes, but for this project I have chosen the 'Nelly Moser', as the petals are such striking shades of pink.

The instructions:

1. Cut 30in (75cm) of 28-gauge purple or silver wire. Find the centre and make a 1¼in (3cm) long loop. As with all wire petals, twist the wire three times to secure.

2. Continue until you have made a further seven loops. Finish off the spare wire by twisting the two pieces together at the back of the flower to form the stem.

3. The centre for this flower is different from the Basic Flower:

   a. Cut 6in (15cm) of 34-gauge silver wire. Join one end of the wire to the stem by wrapping it around, and bring the other end to the top of the flower.
   b. Thread eight embroidery/seed beads onto the wire and allow them to drop to the centre of the flower, arranging them in a circle.
   c. To secure, take the wire down underneath the flower between two petals and back up to the top again on the other side between two petals.
   d. Thread approximately 15–20 pink beads (depending whether you use embroidery or seed, as they vary in size). Place them in a circle around the yellow beads. Add or subtract the beads until they sit neatly.
   e. Take the end of the wire and thread it through the first bead to secure the circle. Take the wire down to the back of the flower and wrap the remainder around the stem. Cut off the excess.

You will need:

Wirecraft
30in (75cm) 28-gauge purple or silver wire

6in (15cm) 34-gauge silver wire

Approx. 8 yellow embroidery or seed beads

15–20 pink embroidery/seed beads

Pale pink mulberry paper

Deep pink felt-tipped pen

Pastel chalks (optional)

Approx. 25 green embroidery/seed beads for stem (optional)

Card
8½ x 8¼in (22 x 21cm) pink card

4¾ x 4in (12 x 10cm) pink card

5 x 4¼in (12.5 x 10.5cm) white card

4¼ x 3¼in (11 x 8.5cm) white card

4½ x 3½in (11.5 x 9cm) green card

Leaf-shaped stamp

Green ink pad

White ink pad

1

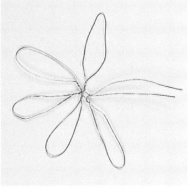

2

4

6

4. To shape the petals, first squeeze the tip of each petal with your finger and thumb. Next, with finger and thumb on both sides of the wire half way down, gently pull open to the desired shape. Continue in the same way with all eight petals.

5. Cut eight pieces of mulberry paper larger than each petal and attach them one at a time, as described in the Basic Flower (see steps 9–11, page 22).

6. To complete the clematis, gently colour down the centre of each petal with a deep pink pen (see Tip below).

7. Finish the stem, as described in the Basic Flower (see step 12, pages 22–23).

To make the card:

1. Score and fold in half a piece of pink card measuring 8½ x 8¼in (22 x 21cm).
2. Stamp the front of the card with a leaf-shaped stamp using white ink.
3. Cut and glue a piece of plain white card measuring 5 x 4¼in (12.5 x 10.5cm).
4. Cut and glue a piece of plain pink card measuring 4¾ x 4in (12 x 10cm).
5. Cut and glue a piece of plain green card measuring 4½ x 3½in (11.5 x 9cm).
6. Cut plain white card measuring 4¼ x 3¼in (11 x 8.5cm).
7. Stamp the white card with the leaf stamp in green ink.
8. Finally, glue the white card onto the green card and attach the clematis.

Tip

Before colouring the petals, experiment with pastel chalks and/or different types of felt-tipped pens and crayons on a spare piece of mulberry paper until you are happy with your choice of colours.

Pansy & Honesty

This dainty pansy design would make a lovely thank you or birthday card. Pansies are often two-toned with the upper petals a different colour from the larger lower petal, so although you will use the same colour wire throughout, it is nice to choose two colours of mulberry paper.

Pansy & Honesty

The instructions:

1. Cut 18in (45cm) of 28-gauge purple or copper wire. Starting in the centre of the wire form a small circle (not a loop) with a diameter of ¾in (2cm). Twist the circle three times to secure. Working with the wire from the left, make two more petals in the same way.

2. Using the right-hand wire, make one more small circle and a large loop measuring 1¼in (3cm) across, which will form the lower petal. Arrange the four small petals at the top of the flower, overlapping each one slightly, and position the larger one at the bottom.

3. Twist the remaining wire together at the back then shape the larger petal with your finger and thumb by pushing the top of it slightly over the base of the four small petals.

4. Cut 6in (15cm) of 34-gauge purple or copper wire and wrap it around the stem to attach. Bring the wire up to the top between the large lower petal and the small petal, either on the left or the right.

You will need:

Wirecraft
Pansy:

18in (45cm) 28-gauge purple or copper wire

6in (15cm) 34-gauge purple or copper wire

Approx. 6 yellow embroidery beads

Lilac mulberry paper

White mulberry paper

Felt-tipped pens

Honesty:

18in (45cm) 34-gauge silver wire

Silver webbing

Card

8½ x 4¼in (22 x 11cm) white card

4 x 4in (10.5 x 10.5cm) handmade paper

Decorative-edged scissors

Purple ribbon

Tip

To create a realistic pansy, copy one from real life or from a gardening book. It will help you to arrange the top petals, which vary in how they sit depending on the variety of pansy.

28

1

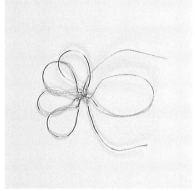

2

3

6

To make the card:

1. Score and fold a piece of white card measuring 8½ x 4¼in (22 x 11cm).

2. Cut handmade paper measuring 4 x 4in (10.5 x 10.5cm) and trim the corners with decorative-edged scissors. Glue to the card.

3. Attach the pansy, honesty and a ribbon.

5. Thread three yellow embroidery beads, dropping them down one at a time over the centre (see Basic Flower, step 6, page 21 for instructions). Take the wire down underneath the flower and back up to the front again, thread three more beads and repeat. Rearrange the petals now if necessary.

6. Cut four pieces of lilac mulberry paper and one piece of white (or your chosen colour scheme). Glue and attach as described in the Basic Flower (see steps 9–11, page 22).

7. To complete the pansy colour in the petals as illustrated or copy a real pansy. Finish the stem as described in the Basic Flower (see step 12, pages 22–23).

Tip

It can be effective to add additional colours and markings to the petals with felt-tipped pens. Practise on a spare piece of mulberry paper first to ensure you like the colours.

8

9

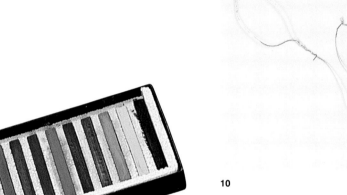

10

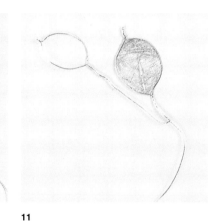

11

8. To make the honesty, cut 18in (45cm) of 34-gauge silver wire. Starting at one end of the wire form a loop that is 1¼in (3cm) long. Overlap the wire so that ¾in (2cm) of spare wire sits over the main wire. Twist the loop three times.

9. Continue twisting the spare piece of wire around the main wire for approximately ¾in (2cm).

10. 2¼in (6cm) down the wire form another 1¼in (3cm) loop. Twist the wire three times and then continue twisting down the stem for a further 1¼in (3cm) – this will form the stem for that leaf. If there is enough wire, repeat again for a third leaf. Pinch the tips of each loop, twisting the points between your finger and thumb for about ¼in (1cm).

11. Cut two or three pieces of silver webbing ribbon (depending on the number of petals) and attach to the wire.

Purple Pansy

To make the card:

1. Score and fold pink card measuring 8¼ x 5¾in (21 x 14.5cm).

2. Cut a piece of pretty backing paper measuring 4 x 3in (10 x 8cm) (I have used a pansy print). Glue to the top half of the card.

3. Cut a piece of dotted parchment paper measuring 5½ x 4in (14 x 10cm) and cut the edge with deckle-edged scissors.

4. Glue the part of the parchment that will be covered with the pansy, as parchment tends to show the glue through the paper. Use peel-off hearts to attach the corners to the card.

5. Cut a piece of purple webbing measuring 2 x 2in (5 x 5cm). Thread the thin stem of the pansy through the webbing and attach both together with glue dots.

You will need:

Wirecraft
18in (45cm) 28-gauge purple wire

6in (15cm) 34-gauge purple wire

Approx. 6 yellow embroidery beads

Lilac mulberry paper

Purple mulberry paper

Card
8¼ x 5¾in (21 x 14.5cm) pink card

4 x 3in (10 x 8cm) backing paper

5½ x 4in (14 x 10cm) dotted parchment paper

Peel-off hearts

2 x 2in (5 x 5cm) purple webbing

Deckle-edged scissors

Glue dots

Lilac Clematis

The 'Jackmanii' is another easy clematis to copy, especially as it only has four petals. The flower is in fact a deep purple but unfortunately if you are not careful any excess glue that you might have left behind will show up on dark purple paper, so I have chosen a lighter shade.

The instructions:

1. Cut 18in (45cm) of 28-gauge purple wire and make a loop that is 1¼in (3cm) long. Twist three times.

2. Make three more loops then take the spare wire to the back and twist to form the stem.

3. Cut 6in (15cm) of 34-gauge purple wire and wrap it around the stem to attach. Bring the wire up between the petals to the front. Add one large brown bead, placing it in the centre of the flower.

4. Take the wire down between two opposite petals and back up to the front again. Thread approximately ten smaller brown, gold and purple beads to encircle the large bead, then thread the end of the wire through the first bead to secure the circle. Take the wire down to the back and twist around the stem. Trim the excess.

5. To shape the petals, squeeze the points with your finger and thumb then half way down pull open gently. Widen the end of the petal near the centre just a little.

6. Cut four pieces of purple mulberry paper and complete the flower and stem as described in the Basic Flower (see steps 9–12, pages 22–23).

You will need:

Wirecraft

18in (45cm) 28-gauge purple wire

6in (15cm) 34-gauge purple wire

One large brown bead

Approx. 10 small beads (brown, gold and purple)

Lilac mulberry paper

Card

8½ x 8¼in (22 x 21cm) white card

7½ x 3½in (19 x 9cm) white card

8 x 4in (20 x 10cm) purple card

Decorative corner punch

To make the card:

1. Score and fold white card measuring 8½ x 8¼in (22 x 21cm).

2. Cut and glue purple card measuring 8 x 4in (20 x 10cm).

3. Cut white card measuring 7½ x 3½in (19 x 9cm). Punch the corners then glue to the purple card.

4. Glue the flower and leaves onto the card (instructions for leaves are on page 51).

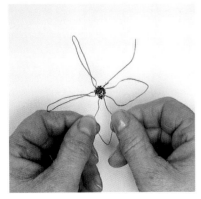

5

Red Poppy

I love to see a field of poppies; it is such a visually uplifting sight. The inspiration for this card came from one such field near my home.

The pretty silver material and sparkling red sequin waste combine to create a lovely effect that complements this red poppy perfectly.

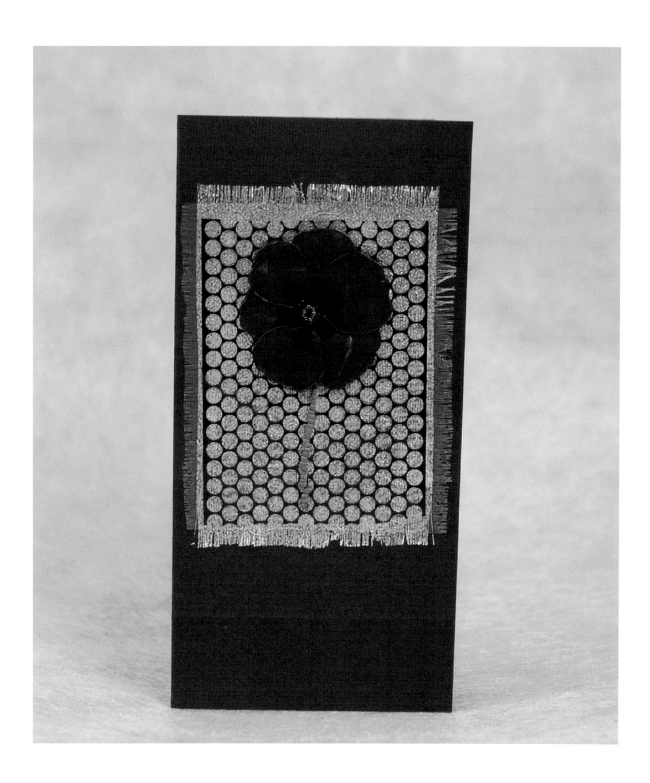

The instructions:

1. Cut 24in (60cm) of red 28-gauge wire. Starting at one end of the wire form a circle with a diameter of ¾in (2cm). Twist three times to secure.

2. Continue to make five more petals. Take the wire to the back and twist to secure and form the stem.

3. Cut 8in (20cm) of 34-gauge silver or gold wire and wrap it around the stem to attach. Bring the wire up to the front of the flower and thread a small black bead. Hold it in the centre while you thread the wire down under the flower and back up to the front again.

4. Thread eight to ten small green beads (the amount will depend on the size of your beads, but you will need enough to form a circle around the first one). Thread the end of the wire through the first bead in the circle. Again, take the wire down underneath and back up to the front. Thread enough black beads to surround the green beads and secure at the back of the flower.

5. Shape the petals by crimping gently with your fingertips or a pair of scissors and arrange the poppy petals so that three sit underneath three top petals.

You will need:

Wirecraft
24in (60cm) 28-gauge red wire

8in (20cm) 34-gauge silver or gold wire

8–10 small green beads

Approx. 15 small black beads

Red mulberry paper

Black felt-tipped pen

Approx. 30 green embroidery beads for stem (optional)

Card
8½ x 8¼in (22 x 21cm) red card

5 x 3¾in (12.5 x 9.5cm) silver material

4¼ x 3in (10.5 x 8cm) red sequin waste

Metal glue

Tip
Dried glue tends to show up on red mulberry paper, so be extra careful when gluing!

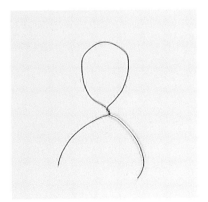

1

4

5

6. Cut six rectangular pieces of red mulberry paper, ensuring that each piece is larger than the wire petals.

7. Turn the flower over so the back is facing you. With a piece of kitchen paper to hand, carefully apply a very thin strip of glue around one petal then immediately use the kitchen paper to remove any excess glue.

8. Quickly place one of the pieces of mulberry paper to the underside of the petal frame, pressing gently between your fingers and thumb.

9. Turn the flower back over to the front and with shaped scissors trim away the excess paper as close to the wire frame as possible. Continue in the same way, completing one petal at a time.

10. Use a black felt-tipped pen to mark the centre of each petal (see Tip below).

11. As the stem of a poppy is very thick and fleshy I have chosen to thread it with green beads. Secure the end of the wire by threading it through the last bead a second time then cut off the excess wire.

To make the card:

1. Score and fold red card measuring 8½ x 8¼in (22 x 21cm).

2. Cut a piece of silver material measuring 5 x 3¾in (12.5 x 9.5cm). Fray the edges then glue to the front of the card.

3. Cut a piece of red sequin waste measuring 4 x 3in (10.5 x 8cm) and glue with metal glue to the material.

4. Glue the poppy to the card.

Tip
As the petals overlap each other it makes it difficult to attach the paper, so you will need to bend each petal gently out of the way while you work.

Tip
When colouring the petals, remember to try the pen on a spare piece of red mulberry paper until you are happy with the effect. Look in a gardening book to see the correct markings.

Lampshade Poppy

There are several varieties of lampshade poppy in my gardening book, ranging from yellow and orange through to blue.

This particular lampshade poppy has the latin name of *Meconopsis integrifolia*. I think it is a stunning variety in this bright shade of yellow.

The instructions:

1. Cut 32in (80cm) of 28-gauge gold wire. Starting in the middle of the wire, form two circles with a diameter of 1¼in (3cm) and secure.

2. Keeping the wire at the top, make two more 1¼in (3cm) circles and four smaller circles, each with a diameter of ¾in (2cm). Secure the spare wire at the back by twisting to form the stem.

3. Attach 6in (15cm) of 34-gauge gold wire by wrapping it around the stem. Thread a large yellow bead and hold it in the centre while you secure it in place. Thread enough small yellow beads to encircle the large bead. Secure the wire at the back.

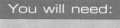

You will need:

Wirecraft

32in (80cm) 28-gauge gold wire

6in (15cm) 34-gauge gold wire

One large yellow bead

Approx. 12 small yellow beads

Yellow mulberry paper

Card

8½ x 8¼in (22 x 21cm) cream card

6¾ x 2¾in (17 x 7cm) cream card

7½ x 3¼in (19 x 8.5cm) yellow pearlized card

5½ x 1½in (14 x 4cm) pale green webbing

Gold thread

Decorative corner punch

Yellow organza ribbon

Deckle-edged scissors

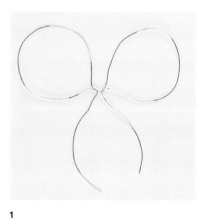

1

2

3

4. Take some time to shape the petals, as illustrated.

a. Pinch the ends of the petals to a rounded point
b. Pull out the lower ends of the petals to widen
c. Crinkle the top

5. Cut eight pieces of yellow mulberry paper. Glue to the wire petals then finish the stem as described in the Basic Flower (see steps 9–12, pages 22–23).

To make the card:

1. Score and fold cream card measuring 8½ x 8¼in (22 x 21cm).

2. Cut yellow pearlized card measuring 7½ x 3¼in (19 x 8.5cm). Punch the corners and add two strands of gold thread for decoration. Glue to the front of the card.

3. Cut cream card measuring 6¾ x 2¾in (17 x 7cm). Deckle the edges then glue to the yellow card.

4. Cut 5½ x 1½in (14 x 4cm) of green webbing and attach to centre of the cream card.

5. Glue the poppy to the webbing and add a bow.

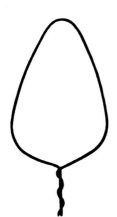

a

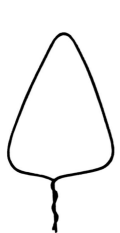

b

c

Poinsettia

The poinsettia is such a beautiful Christmas plant, and comes in more than one colour. Here I show how to make the traditional red and the gold, but if you would like to make the cream version I suggest you use green or silver wire and cream or white mulberry paper. The poinsettia is fairly difficult to make as their are 12 bracts, which when you come to the gluing can get very messy, so don't attempt this one until you're confident!

The instructions:

1. Cut 36in (90cm) of 28-gauge red wire. Starting at one end of the wire, make four loops that are 1¼in (3cm) long. Keep the wire at the top of the flower then make four more loops that are 1¼in (3cm) long. Make a further four ½in (1.5cm) long loops (three if you haven't enough wire). Secure the wire at the back by twisting to form the stem.

Tip
Not only can you make a Christmas card with the poinsettia and holly leaves, they can also be used to decorate name-settings or candles for a festive table display.

2. Attach 6in (15cm) of 34-gauge gold wire by wrapping it around the stem. Add four seed beads in yellow. Keeping them in position on top as much as possible, take the wire down underneath and back up to the top again. Add a few more yellow beads and a few red and green alternately to give the appearance of tiny flowers in the centre.

3. Shape each bract by pinching the tip between your fingers and then gently pulling apart again.

4. Cut 12 pieces of red mulberry paper larger than each bract and then glue them in turn (see Basic Flower, steps 9–12, pages 22–23). You will have to gently move them out of the way to reach them all.

5. For this flower, I have cut off the stem.

Tip
Remember to be careful when gluing – red paper can show the dried glue!

1

2 & 3

Tip

When attaching transparent ribbon or paper it is important not to allow the glue to show through. This is why I have used stars to attach the ribbon to the paper.

To make the card:

1. Score and fold a piece of red card measuring 8¼ x 6in (21 x 15cm).

2. Cut a piece of glossy gold card measuring 3½ x 2¾in (9 x 7cm) and glue to the centre of the red card.

3. Fix a piece of black webbing measuring 5¾ x 4in (14.5 x 10cm) onto the gold card where the poinsettia will sit to avoid the glue showing.

4. Attach the poinsettia.

5. Glue tiny stars to the corners with small glue dots, pressing down firmly so that the glue goes through the webbing to the card underneath.

Wirecraft
Poinsettia:

36in (90cm) 28-gauge gold wire

6in (15cm) 34-gauge gold wire

Approx. 15 red seed beads

Gold webbing

Holly:

18in (45cm) 28-gauge
   green wire

6in (15cm) 34-gauge
   green wire

Green mulberry paper

0.5 fine green ink pen

Green pastel chalks

Card
8¼ x 6in (21 x 15cm) green card

5 x 3½in (12.5 x 9cm) green
   mulberry paper

4¾ x 3¼in (12 x 8.5cm) white
   mulberry paper

4 x 2¾in (10 x 7cm) red card

4 x 2½in (10 x 6.5cm)
   gold mesh

I have added holly to this design for an extra festive touch.

To make the holly:

1. Cut 18in (45cm) of 28-gauge green wire. Fold the wire in half and pinch the fold with your finger and thumb to make a point. Make a 1½in (4cm) long loop and twist.

2. Separate the wires, one to the left and one to the right, and make a 1½in (4cm) long loop on each side (you will have about 1¼in (3cm) of wire left over). You should now have three long loops and a 1¼in (3cm) tail. Pinch the ends of the other two points as before. Twist the two spare pieces together to secure, or twist for only ¼in (1cm) and curl, as illustrated.

3. Starting with one of the loops, shape into a holly leaf. You will need to pinch the wire three times on either side of the leaf. If you have trouble getting the shape right, practise on some spare wire. Do the same with the other two loops.

4. Cut 6in (15cm) of 34-gauge green wire and attach to the stem. Thread approximately 15 red beads or five to six large red beads (to look like berries) and wrap the wire around the base of the three leaves, keeping the beads to the front. Finish off the spare wire around the stem.

5. Cut three pieces of green mulberry paper and attach to the wire leaves. To make them look more realistic I have used a fine green ink pen (0.5) to draw the veins and used green pastel chalks for extra colour.

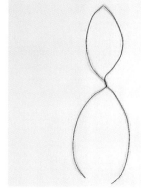

1

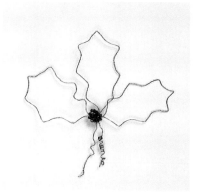

3

Wet-tearing

To wet-tear, use a wet, clean paintbrush to draw the shape you require on your mulberry paper, then gently tear apart.

To make the card:

1. Score and fold green card measuring 8¼ x 6in (21 x 15cm).

2. Wet-tear (see instructions above) green mulberry paper measuring 5 x 3½in (12.5 x 9cm). Glue to the card.

3. Wet-tear white mulberry paper measuring 4¾ x 3¼in (12 x 8.5cm) and glue to the green card.

4. Cut a piece of red card measuring 4 x 2¾in (10 x 7cm).

5. Glue a piece of gold mesh measuring 4 x 2¾in (10 x 7cm) to the red card and attach to the white mulberry paper.

6. Attach the holly leaves with glue and then finally attach the poinsettia.

Pink Flower

This card has a young and contemporary feel to it and would be suitable for celebrating a wide variety of occasions. Rather than copying a real flower, I decided to have fun inventing this one. You could do the same. Try experimenting with tiny flowers and different beads, or perhaps multicoloured or alternate-coloured petals. Be as extravagant and creative as you like!

You will need:

Wirecraft

14in (35cm) 28-gauge
   copper wire

8in (20cm) 34-gauge copper wire

One large green bead

Approx. 10 small yellow beads

Pink mulberry paper

Deep pink/purple felt-tipped pen

Card

8¼ x 6in (21 x 15cm) pink card

5½ x 3¾in (14 x 9.5cm)
   black card

Daisy punch

Glue dots

The instructions:

1. Cut 14in (35cm) of 28-gauge copper wire.

2. Form six circles with ¾in (2cm) diameters.

3. Join 8in (20cm) of 34-gauge copper wire to the stem at the back and bring to the front.

4. Thread a green bead in the centre and surround it by a circle of yellow beads. Secure in place.

5. Shape the petals by pinching them gently at the points and then carefully pulling them open again half way down on each side.

6. Cut six pieces of pink mulberry paper and attach them to the wire petals (see Basic Flower, steps 9–11, pages 22–23).

7. Colour the base of each petal with a deep pink or purple felt-tipped pen.

8. Cut the stem and curl.

6

To make the card:

1. Score and fold a piece of pink card measuring 8¼ x 6in (21 x 15cm).

2. Cut a piece of black card measuring 5½ x 3¾in (14 x 9.5cm) and punch daisy shapes around the edge of the card. Glue into place.

3. Attach the flower with glue dots.

Moth Orchid

I love orchids, especially the moth orchid, which flowers for up to three months at a time. It is, however, by far the most difficult flower to make, and to describe how to make it is equally hard, so I hope by now you are able to understand my instructions – here goes!

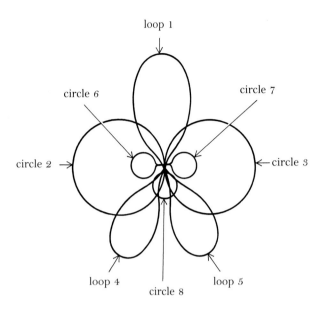

loop 1

circle 6

circle 7

circle 2

circle 3

loop 4

loop 5

circle 8

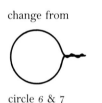

change from

to

circle 6 & 7

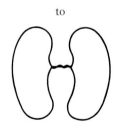

change from

to

circle 8

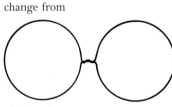

change from

to

circles 2 & 3

The instructions:

1. Cut 28in (70cm) of 28-gauge gold wire. In the centre, form a circle with a 1¼in (3cm) diameter. Make a second 1¼in (3cm) circle (see circles 2 and 3 and picture 1).

2. In between the two circles, form a loop that is 1⅜in (3.5cm) long (see loop 1). Form a smaller loop 1¼in (3cm) long under the left-hand circle (see loop 4 and picture 2) and a second under the right-hand circle (see loop 5).

3. Bring the wire up to the front between loop 1 and circle 2 and make a circle with a diameter of ¼in (1cm) (see circle 6 and picture 3a). Always twist the wire in between to secure. Take the wire down to the back and up between loop 1 and circle 3 and form another ¼in (1cm) circle (see circle 7 and picture 3b). Take the wire down to the back again and up between loops 4 and 5. Form a circle with a ½in (1.5cm) diameter (see circle 8 and picture 3c). Take the leftover wire to the back and twist together to create a stem.

4. Cut 6in (15cm) of 34-gauge gold wire and attach it to the stem. Bring it up through the circles to the front. Thread pink and yellow embroidery beads then wrap around the centre. Shape the petals as illustrated on the facing page.

5. Cut eight pieces of white mulberry paper, each larger than the petals, then attach as usual, bending the others out of the way while you work.

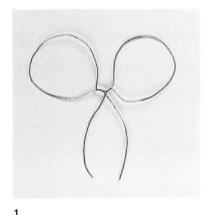

1

2

3a

3b

3c & 4

To make the card:

1. Score and fold a piece of white card measuring 8½ x 8¼in (22 x 21cm).

2. Wet-tear (see page 44) pink mulberry paper measuring 8 x 4in (20 x 10cm) and glue to the white card.

3. Wet-tear another piece of pink mulberry paper measuring 4¾ x 3½in (12 x 9cm) and glue to the top of the card.

4. Stamp a rubber stamp design of your choice onto a piece of white card measuring 4 x 2¾in (10 x 7cm) using black ink and then colour with pencils. Glue to the mulberry paper.

5. Cut pink pearlized card measuring 2½ x 1⅜in (6.5 x 3.5cm) and trim with deckle-edged scissors. Attach to the centre of the stamped card.

6. Glue the orchid to the card then finish by decorating with a few heart-shaped stickers.

You will need:

Wirecraft

28in (70cm) 28-gauge gold wire

6in (15cm) 34-gauge gold wire

1 yellow and approx. 8 red embroidery beads

Yellow mulberry paper

Card

11 x 5½in (28 x 14cm) cream card

4½ x 4½in (11.5 x 11.5cm) cream card

5¼ x 5¼in (13 x 13cm) yellow mulberry paper

Flower or leaf stamp

Coloured pencils

Glue dots

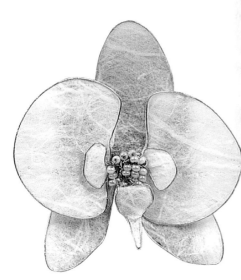

To make the card:

1. Score and fold in half a piece of cream card measuring 11 x 5½in (28 x 14cm).

2. Wet-tear (see page 44) and glue a piece of yellow mulberry paper measuring 5¼ x 5¼in (13 x 13cm) to the front of the card.

3. Cut a piece of cream card that is 4½ x 4½in (11.5 x 11.5cm), stamp with a suitable flower or leaf stamp then glue to the front. Colour your stamped design with coloured pencils.

4. Attach the orchid with glue dots.

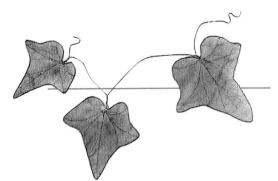

Leaves

Once you have mastered the flowers, you should be able to make a selection of leaves. Just look in a gardening book or take a leaf from the garden and copy. For spring and summer you could use green wire and the many shades of green that mulberry paper comes in, and for autumn, copper wire and mulberry paper in oranges, browns and reds would be very effective.

There are two ways to make the leaves:

1. Make a loop in the wire and twist three times, as with the flowers. Shape the wires to your chosen leaf shape and then cover with mulberry paper.

2. Cut two pieces of green mulberry paper, measuring approximately 4 x 1¼in (10 x 3cm) (a). Add glue to one of the pieces. Place a length of wire in the centre of the glued mulberry paper and then place the second piece directly on top (b). The wire will be held in position, allowing you to trim the paper to the shape of a leaf with deckle-edged scissors (c).

2a

2b

2c

Insects

In this chapter you will find pretty dragonflies, butterflies and a charming bumble bee card. They are ideal to send to both men and women; a pastel-coloured card or a black and white background is all that is needed to make them more masculine or feminine. Once you become really competent at wirecraft, there are, of course, many other insects that you could make.

Dragonfly

Dragonflies are beautiful creatures and make a lovely motif for a card. Their wings show such a multitude of colours when they catch the light, that you could choose almost any combination of colours for your wirecraft and it would look realistic, so have fun experimenting!

The instructions:

1. Cut 12in (30cm) of 34-gauge silver wire (28-gauge is not delicate enough for this purpose). Thread one opalescent bead for the body onto the wire. Bend the wire in the centre so that the bead sits in the middle.

2. Thread a second bead onto either side of the wire and hold it between your finger and thumb about ⅜in (2cm) from the end of the wire. Push the wire (the one without the second bead) through the second bead (a) and gently pull both wires, easing the bead evenly down to sit on top of the first bead (b, c).

3. Continue until you have approximately eight beads threaded (depending on the size of your beads). Thread both wires through one longer or oval bead (you may need to trim one end off to make the ends the same length for ease of threading), divide the wires again, then thread one small bead, as before, for the head. To finish the wires, either twist them around a cocktail stick or gently bend for antennae.

You will need:

Wirecraft
12in (30cm) 34-gauge silver wire

12in (30cm) 28-gauge silver wire

One double-length or oval bead

Approx. 8 small opalescent beads

1 pearlized small bead

White mulberry paper

Card
12 x 6in (30 x 15cm) white card

5¼ x 5¼in (13.5 x 13.5cm) black card

5 x 5in (13 x 13cm) black gingham backing paper

4¼ x 4¼in (11 x 11cm) black card

4 x 4in (10.5 x 10.5cm) white card

3 x 3in (8 x 8cm) black mulberry paper

Dragonfly-shaped stamp

Black ink pad

1

2a

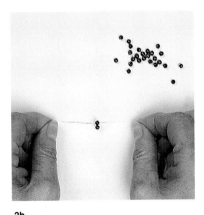

2b

2c

3

4

4. Cut 12in (30cm) of 28-gauge silver wire and fold in half. Wrap the folded wire twice around the body in between the head and the body to secure in place. On one side of the wire make a 1½in (4cm) long loop. Holding the join of the loop really close to the body, twist it three times to secure. Make a second wing on the other side. Make a second smaller wing that is 1¼in (3cm) long on either side, then twist to secure.

5. Use the leftover pieces of wire – they should be ¾–1¼in (2–3cm) long – as legs or cut off if not wanted. Readjust the wings to a pleasing shape.

6. Cut four pieces of white mulberry paper and attach, as described in the Basic Flower (see steps 9–11, page 22).

Tip

As an alternative to mulberry paper you can use webbing ribbon for the wings.

To make the card:

1. Score and fold white card measuring 12 x 6in (30 x 15cm).

2. Cut and glue black card measuring 5¼ x 5¼in (13.5 x 13.5cm).

3. Cut and glue black gingham backing paper measuring 5 x 5in (13 x 13cm).

4. Cut and glue black card measuring 4¼ x 4¼in (11 x 11cm).

5. Cut a piece of white card measuring 4 x 4in (10.5 x 10.5cm). Stamp with dragonfly-shaped stamp and glue into place.

6. Wet-tear (see page 44 for instructions) a piece of black mulberry paper measuring 3 x 3in (8 x 8cm) square and glue to the dragonfly-stamped card.

7. Glue the dragonfly in place with a glue dot.

You will need:

Wirecraft

12in (30cm) 34-gauge silver wire

12in (30cm) 28-gauge wire

One double-length or oval bead

Approx. 11 blue
  embroidery beads

1 small pearlized bead

Turquoise blue mulberry paper

Card

8½ x 8¼in (22 x 21cm)
  turquoise card

Cream webbing

Decorative square punch

Glue dots

To make the card:

1. Score and fold in half a piece of turquoise card measuring 8½ x 8¼in (22 x 21cm).

2. Punch a large hole with a decorative square punch.

3. Attach a square piece of cream webbing to the underneath of the square.

4. Punch a square of a floral design paper with the same punch and glue to the inside of the card so that it shows through the window.

5. Attach the dragonfly to the webbing with glue dots.

Pink Dragonfly

You will need:

Wirecraft

12in (30cm) 34-gauge gold wire

12in (30cm) 28-gauge gold wire

One double-length or oval bead

9 small pink pearlized beads

1 small black pearlized bead

Pink mulberry paper

Card

12 x 6in (30 x 15cm) cream card

4¾ x 4¾in (12 x 12cm) pink card

Handmade paper

Deckle-edged scissors

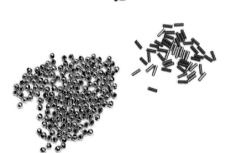

To make the card:

1. Cut and fold in half a piece of cream card measuring 12 x 6in (30 x 15cm).

2. Cut and glue a piece of pink card measuring 4¾ x 4¾in (12 x 12cm).

3. Punch out 2in (5cm) squares from handmade paper, deckle the edges then glue to 2in (5cm) squares of cream card.

4. Overlap and glue the squares in place.

5. Glue the dragonfly onto the card with glue dots.

Butterfly

Butterflies vary so much in their colours and markings. I decided to create my own but you could look through a wildlife book and copy your favourite species. To add a bit of sparkle you could decorate it with glitter or sequins, or perhaps use some ribbon for the wings.

Butterfly

The instructions:

1. Cut 8in (20cm) of 34-gauge silver wire and thread your chosen beads in the same way as the dragonfly (see steps 1–2, page 55) – this time only seven beads are needed, though. Trim the ends of the wires to make them the same length and thread them through one larger round bead for the head. Thread a tiny bead onto each wire and secure by re-threading.

2. Cut 8in (20cm) of 28-gauge silver wire and bend it gently in half. Secure the wire to the body by wrapping it twice between the head bead and the end of the body. Form a circle with a ¾in (2cm) diameter on either side of the body. Twist each circle twice.

You will need:

Wirecraft
8in (20cm) 34-gauge silver wire

8in (20cm) 28-gauge silver wire

2 tiny cream pearlized beads

7 small cream pearlized beads

1 medium-sized cream pearlized bead

Pink mulberry paper

Card
8¼ x 6in (21 x 15cm) cream pearlized card

5½ x 4in (14 x 10cm) pink card

5¼ x 3¾in (13.5 x 9.5cm) handmade paper

Flower stamp

Cream backing paper

Yellow accent beads

Glue dot

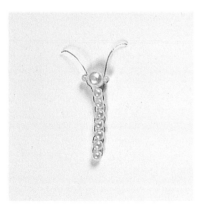

1

2

3

3. Make two more circles, slightly smaller at ½in (1.5cm), for the lower wings. Trim the spare wire or twist slightly to create back legs. Now mould the wings to your desired shape.

4. Cut four pieces of pink mulberry paper and glue to the wings (see the Basic Flower, Steps 9–11, page 22).

To make the card:

1. Score and fold in half a piece of cream pearlized card measuring 8¼ x 6in (21 x 15cm).

2. Cut and glue a piece of pink card measuring 5½ x 4in (14 x 10cm).

3. Cut and glue handmade paper measuring 5¼ x 3¾in (13.5 x 9.5cm).

4. Stamp two flowers on a spare piece of backing paper. Cut them out and glue them in layers to the front of the card.

5. Glue yellow accent beads to the flower centre.

6. Attach the butterfly with glue dots.

Tip

Accent beads are tiny beads without holes that can be used to accentuate a project. Place some glue in the area you wish to decorate then sprinkle the beads. Shake off the excess and leave to dry for a few hours.

You will need:

Wirecraft

8in (20cm) 34-gauge silver wire

8in (20cm) 28-gauge silver wire

2 tiny blue pearlized beads

8 small black beads

1 medium-sized black pearlized bead

Green mulberry paper

Blue felt-tipped pen

Card

12 x 6in (30 x 15cm) white card

4 x 4in (10 x 10cm) green card

3¾ x 3¾in (9.5 x 9.5cm) gold card

3½ x 3½in (9 x 9cm) white handmade paper

Lightbox

Embossing tool

Daisy punch

Deckle-edged scissors

Yellow accent beads

Glue dot

To make the card:

1. Score and fold white card measuring 12 x 6in (30 x 15cm).

2. Dry emboss a 4¼ x 4¼in (11 x 11cm) frame using a lightbox and embossing tool (see right for instructions).

3. Cut and glue green card measuring 4 x 4in (10 x 10cm).

4. Cut and glue gold card measuring 3¾ x 3¾in (9.5 x 9.5cm).

5. Cut then deckle edge and glue white handmade paper measuring 3½ x 3½in (9 x 9cm).

6. Punch out six small daisies then glue together, overlapping their petals.

7. Glue yellow accent beads to the centre of each flower then glue to the card.

8. Attach the butterfly with a glue dot.

Dry Embossing

1. Place a stencil onto a lightbox with tape to hold it in place.

2. Place your card right side down on the stencil.

3. With your embossing tool, gently press the card onto the stencil.

4. When you turn the card the right side up the image will be embossed.

Bumble Bee

Bumble bees are always drawn to the flowers in my garden and look so attractive nestled among the brightly coloured petals that I was inspired to make this card. The striking red three-dimensional flower complements and draws attention to the delicate wirecraft bee.

Bumble Bee

The instructions:

Tip

If you haven't threaded beads in this way before, I suggest you try making the dragonfly on pages 54–58 or butterfly on pages 59–62 first.

1. Cut 12in (30cm) of 34-gauge silver wire and thread three white beads onto the centre of the wire (bend the wire slightly in the centre so that they remain in place). Thread four black beads onto one side of the wire. Try to hold the beads between your finger and thumb so that they don't drop down to the white ones.

2. Thread the other wire (the one without the black beads) through the four black beads. The process is exactly the same as for the dragonfly and butterfly (see pages 54–56 and 59–61) except that you work with more than one bead at a time. Pull both wires, letting the beads sit on top of the row of white ones.

3. Thread and knit four white beads.

4. Thread and knit three black beads.

5. Thread and knit four black beads.

You will need:

Wirecraft
12in (30cm) 34-gauge silver wire x 2

9 white beads

18 black beads

Silver webbing ribbon

Card
12 x 6in (30 x 15cm) white card

5 x 5in (12.5 x 12.5cm) white card

5½ x 5½in (14 x 14cm) red card

Approx. 4 x 4in (10 x 10cm) red card

Leaf stamp

Flower stamp

Green ink pad

Black ink pad

Glue dot

3D foam pads

1

2

Tip

Make sure your beads are exactly the same size, otherwise when you start to 'knit' them together, the amount for each row won't be correct. I have also found that round beads provide a better finish and are easier to use.

6. Thread and knit one black bead, two white, then one black bead again.

7. Thread and knit three black beads.

8. Thread and knit two black beads. Trim the wire, leaving about ¼in (1cm).

9. Form the wings by cutting 12in (30cm) of 34-gauge silver wire. Find the middle and create a loop, measuring about ½in (1.5cm). Twist the wire to secure. Make a second, third and fourth wing. Cut four pieces of silver webbing ribbon and attach as described in the Basic Flower (see steps 9–11, page 22). Glue the wings to the back of the bee with a glue dot before fixing to the card.

8   9

To make the card:

1. Score and fold white card measuring 12 x 6in (30 x 15cm).

2. Cut, tear and glue red card measuring 5½ x 5½in (14 x 14cm).

3. Cut and glue white card measuring 5 x 5in (12.5 x 12.5cm).

4. Stamp the white card with your chosen leaf stamp.

5. Stamp a piece of red card with your chosen flower stamp and a black ink pad twice. Cut out the flower designs and, using 3D foam pads, glue the two pieces together to create a three-dimensional flower. Glue the flower to the card.

6. Attach the bee to the flower with a glue dot.

Funky Wire

These simple yet bold designs can be used for a wide variety of occasions. The thick, textured wires provide quite a fun and quirky feel to the cards. Unlike the designs in the proceeding chapters, many of the projects are formed by wrapping the wires around pencils, pens, lids or matchsticks.

Silver Star

This card has quite a festive feel but could also be sent to celebrate a variety of other occasions. The colours and simple design make it suitable to give to a man or a woman. The silver textured wire, red beads and silver frame catch the light, making it really sparkle!

The instructions:

1. Cut 12in (30cm) of silver textured wire.

2. Form five loops that are exactly the same size, following the instructions for the Basic Flower (see steps 1–3, page 21). Twist the two spare pieces of wire together at the back.

3. To shape the points of the star, follow the instructions for the Lilac Clematis, given on page 32.

4. Join 8in (20cm) of 34-gauge silver wire to the ¾in (2cm) wire at the back. (You will need more than this but if you cut a longer piece it gets tangled, so join some more when needed – see Adding Wire, page 23, for instructions on how to do this.) Bring the wire to the front of the flower.

5. Wrap the wire around the base of one point, thread three red beads, wrap the wire around the tip, re-thread through the three beads, and then wrap once around the base again to secure (a). Repeat with all the points, joining more wire when needed (b).

6. If there is enough wire when you have finished the points, thread as many beads as you like for the centre, following the instructions for the Basic Flower (see steps 4–6, page 21).

You will need:

Wirecraft
12in (30cm) silver textured wire

8in (20cm) 34-gauge silver wire

Approx. 25 red beads

Card
12 x 6in (30 x 15cm) red card

3¾ x 3¾in (9.5 x 9.5cm) silver card

3½ x 3½in (9 x 9cm) red card

2¾ x 2¾in (7.5 x 7.5cm) black card

3 x 3in (7 x 7cm) red card

2½ x 2½in (6.5 x 6.5cm) silver card

2¼ x 2¼in (6 x 6cm) white card

Foam tape

5a

5b

Tip
I used textured wires that are coated in a gold/silver-effect material. If you cannot find textured wires then 24-gauge wires are also suitable.

To make the card:

1. Score and fold red card measuring 12 x 6in (30 x 15cm).

2. Cut and glue silver card measuring 3¾ x 3¾in (9.5 x 9.5cm).

3. Cut and glue red card measuring 3½ x 3½in (9 x 9cm).

4. Cut and glue black card measuring 3 x 3in (7.5 x 7.5cm).

5. Cut and glue red card measuring 2¾ x 2¾in (7 x 7cm).

6. Cut silver card measuring 2½ x 2½in (6.5 x 6.5cm)

7. Cut white card measuring 2¼ x 2¼in (6 x 6cm) and glue to the silver card.

8. Punch a small hole in centre of the white/silver card and thread the long wire through the hole. Trim the wire to ¼in (1cm). Bend the wire over the back and stick with tape to secure.

9. Attach the white/silver card to the centre of the red card with foam tape.

Gold Star

This star was made in exactly the same way as the Silver Star but has six loops not five. The centre is the same as the Lampshade Poppy on page 37.

the Lampshade Poppy on page 37.

You will need:

Wirecraft

12in (30cm) gold textured wire

8in (20cm) 34-gauge gold wire

Approx. 17 pale blue beads

Approx. 11 small dark blue beads

1 large dark blue bead

Card

12 x 6in (30 x 15cm) blue card

4 x 4in (10 x 10cm) white card

4¼ x 4¼in (10.5 x 10.5cm) gold card

Flower stamp

Patterned stamp

Archival Brilliance, Moonlight White ink pad

Archival Brilliance, Pearlescent Sky-blue ink pad

Hole punch

Sticky tape

Gold Star

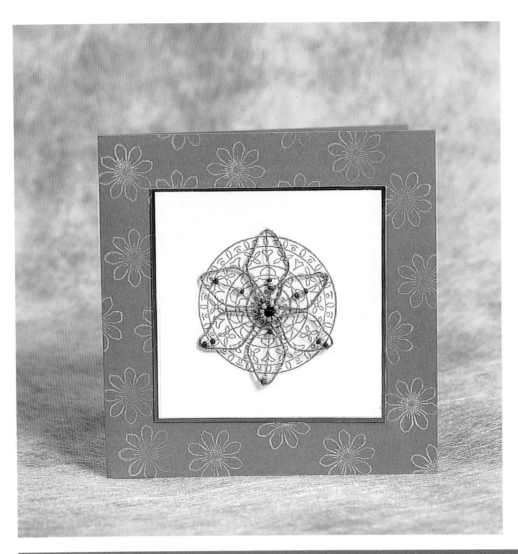

To make the card:

1. Score and fold blue card measuring 12 x 6in (30 x 15cm).

2. Stamp the front of the card with your chosen flower stamp in Archival Brilliance, Moonlight White.

3. Cut and glue gold card measuring 4¼ x 4¼in (10.5 x 10.5cm).

4. Cut white card measuring 4 x 4in (10 x 10cm).

5. Stamp the centre of the card with your chosen patterned stamp in Archival Brilliance, Pearlescent Sky-blue.

6. Punch a small hole through the centre of the pattern and then thread ¾in (2cm) of the wire through the hole. Trim the wire to ¼in (1cm) then bend the wire over the back and stick with tape to secure.

7. Attach white card to the centre of the gold card with tape.

Gold Flower

This simple yet elegant design would make an ideal birthday or greetings card for a multitude of occasions and people of all ages. You can vary the colours and background pattern to suit the recipient, and for extra adornment, add smaller flowers to the corners.

The instructions:

1. Following the instructions for the Basic Flower (see steps 1–3, page 21), cut 10in (25cm) of gold textured wire and form five loops, each measuring ½in (1.5cm) in length.

2. To make the centre, cut 6in (15cm) of 34-gauge gold wire and join it to the stem by wrapping it around. Thread a large pink bead and hold it in the centre while you secure it in place. Thread enough small black beads to encircle the large bead and then secure the wire at the back.

3. Divide the two spare wires at the back and twist them individually.

3

You will need:

Wirecraft

10in (25cm) gold textured wire

6in (15cm) 34-gauge gold wire

12 small black beads

1 large pink pearlized bead

Card

8½ x 8¼in (22 x 21cm) pink card

7½ x 3in (19 x 8cm) backing paper

3½ x 2¼in (9 x 6cm) pink card

Decorative-edged scissors

Glue dot

To make the card:

1. Score and fold a piece of pink card measuring 8½ x 8¼in (22 x 21cm).

2. Cut a piece of backing paper measuring 7½ x 3in (19 x 8cm) and trim the edges with decorative-edged scissors.

3. Cut a piece of pink card measuring 3½ x 2¼in (9 x 6cm), trim the edges again then glue to the card.

4. Glue the flower onto the card with a glue dot.

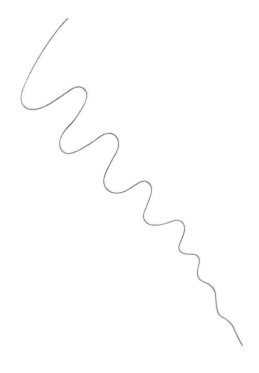

You will need:

Wirecraft

10in (25cm) gold textured wire

6in (15cm) 34-gauge gold wire

1 small blue translucent bead

Card

8½ x 8¼ (22 x 21cm) blue card

8 x 3in (20 x 8cm) blue card

3 x 2in (8 x 5cm) gold
   holographic card

3 x 1¾in (7.5 x 4.5cm) black card

Daisy stamp

Black ink pad

Gold ink pad

Deckle-edged scissors

The instructions:

1. Following the instructions for the Basic Flower (see steps 1–3, page 21), cut 12in (30cm) of gold textured wire and form seven loops, each measuring ½in (1.5cm) in length.

2. Shape the petals by holding a pencil inside the base of the loop and squeezing the tips together. Bend each petal slightly backwards.

3. For the centre, attach 2¼in (6cm) of 34-gauge gold wire and join it to the stem by wrapping it around. Thread a blue bead and hold it in the centre while you secure it in place.

4. Make a curly stem by wrapping the wire around a cocktail stick.

To make the card:

1. Score and fold blue card measuring 8½ x 8¼ (22 x 21cm).

2. Cut another piece of blue card measuring 8 x 3in (20 x 8cm) and stamp with a daisy stamp in black and gold. Glue to the front of the card.

3. Cut gold holographic card measuring 3 x 2in (8 x 5cm) and glue to the top of the card.

4. Cut black card measuring 3 x 1¾in (7.5 x 4.5cm) then trim with deckle-edged scissors and glue to the gold card.

5. Glue the gold flower in place.

Silver Flowers

This is quite a young and fun card that would be ideal to send to a teenage girl. The flowers, which echo the flower-stamped background and create a strong, contemporary theme, are made with silver textured wire. The glass beads provide the finishing touch.

The instructions:

1. Cut a long length of silver textured wire.

2. Starting in the centre of the wire, wrap the wire around a pencil (if you are right-handed, hold the pencil in your right hand and the wire in your left). Hold the join between your finger and thumb of your left hand and turn the pencil clockwise two or three times until a secure circle is formed. Gently remove the pencil. Continue in the same way, making as many circles as the wire allows or you choose. Trim off the excess wire.

3. Attach a different coloured bead to the centre of each flower.

3

You will need:

Wirecraft
Silver textured wire

Pencil

3 large different coloured beads

Card
8½ x 8¼in (22 x 21cm) blue card

7¼ x 3in (18.5 x 7.5cm) blue card

8 x 3½in (20 x 9cm) silver card

7½ x 3¼in (19.5 x 8.5cm) white card

Flower stamp

Black ink pad

Square punch

Glue dots

To make the card:

1. Score and fold blue card measuring 8½ x 8¼in (22 x 21cm).

2. Cut and glue silver card measuring 8 x 3½in (20 x 9cm).

3. Cut and glue white card measuring 7½ x 3¼in (19.5 x 8.5cm).

4. Cut another piece of blue card measuring 7¼ x 3in (18.5 x 7.5cm).

5. Stamp the blue card with your chosen stamp in black ink.

6. Using a 1¼in (3.5cm) square punch, punch three even holes.

7. Glue to the main card.

8. Glue the wire flowers to centre of each square with glue dots.

Bright Flowers

The flowers on this cheerful card are made by wrapping brightly coloured wire around a pencil. Flowers in a vase is a suitable subject to mark many occasions, but I think this card would make a particularly nice Get Well card and will last longer than the real thing.

The instructions:

1. Cut 12in (30cm) of blue wire.

2. Starting in the centre of the wire, wrap the wire around a pencil (if you are right-handed, hold the pencil in your right hand and the wire in your left). Hold the join between your finger and thumb of your left hand and turn the pencil clockwise two or three times until a secure circle is formed. Gently remove the pencil.

3. Continue in the same way, making as many circles as the wire allows or you choose. Finish the wire ends by wrapping them around a cocktail stick.

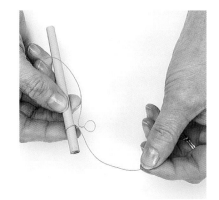

2

Tip

If you wish, you can vary the size of the petals by wrapping the wire around a larger object, such as the lid of a tube or a small glue stick.

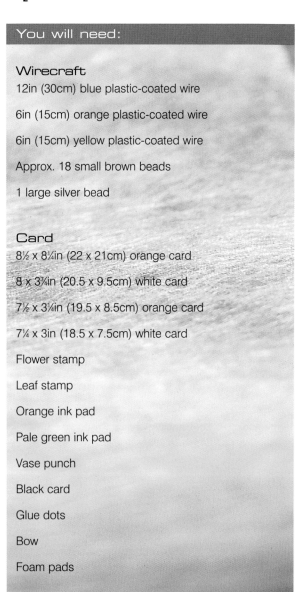

You will need:

Wirecraft

12in (30cm) blue plastic-coated wire

6in (15cm) orange plastic-coated wire

6in (15cm) yellow plastic-coated wire

Approx. 18 small brown beads

1 large silver bead

Card

8½ x 8¼in (22 x 21cm) orange card

8 x 3¾in (20.5 x 9.5cm) white card

7½ x 3¼in (19.5 x 8.5cm) orange card

7¼ x 3in (18.5 x 7.5cm) white card

Flower stamp

Leaf stamp

Orange ink pad

Pale green ink pad

Vase punch

Black card

Glue dots

Bow

Foam pads

4. Cut 6in (15cm) of orange wire. Repeat steps 2 and 3 then wrap the last 4in (10cm) around a cocktail stick to create a curly stem.

5. Cut 6in (15cm) of yellow wire. Again, repeat steps 2 and 3 then wrap the last 4in (10cm) around a cocktail stick to create a curly stem.

6. Attach different coloured beads to the centres, following the instructions given for the Basic Flower (see steps 4–6, page 21).

To make the card:

1. Score and fold in half a piece of orange card measuring 8½ x 8¼in (22 x 21cm).

2. Cut white card measuring 8 x 3¾in (20.5 x 9.5cm) and stamp it with a flower stamp in orange ink and a leaf stamp in pale green ink. Glue to the orange card.

3. Cut and glue orange card measuring 7½ x 3¼in (19.5 x 8.5cm).

4. Cut white card measuring 7¼ x 3in (18.5 x 7.5cm) and glue to the front.

5. Punch a black vase or similar pot and attach with foam pads to raise it from the base of the card.

6. Glue the wire flowers with glue dots, tucking the ends of the wire stem inside the pot.

7. Add a bow or similar to the vase.

Floral Display

When completing these projects you are likely to find that you are left with lots of small pieces of wire. These delicate-looking little flowers are great for using up those leftover bits of wire. It's a very pretty design that would make a lovely Mother's Day or Thank You card.

You will need:

Wirecraft

Silver textured wire

Gold textured wire

3 lilac translucent beads

White wire

Matchstick

Wide pen

Thinner pen

Cocktail stick

Card

8½ x 6in (22 x 15cm) white card

5 x 3in (12.5 x 7.5cm) silver card

5 x 3in (12.5 x 7.5cm) white card

4¾ x 2¾in (12 x 7cm) lilac
  pearlized card

Flower stamp

Lilac ink pad

Corner punch

Glue dots

Lilac bow

The instructions:

1. For each petal, wrap gold or silver textured wire around a matchstick and twist twice.

2. Wire a lilac translucent bead to the centre of each flower.

3. I used white wire for the vase. Start by wrapping the wire around a pen for about six circles, then a smaller pen for a further five circles.

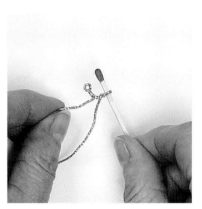

1

4. Wrap the end of the wire around a cocktail stick to finish.

To make the card:

1. Score and fold white card measuring 8½ x 6in (22 x 15cm).

2. Stamp the front of the card with a flower stamp in lilac ink.

3. Cut and glue silver card measuring 5 x 3in (12.5 x 7.5cm).

4. Cut and glue white card measuring 5 x 3in (12.5 x 7.5cm).

5. Cut lilac pearlized card measuring 4¾ x 2¾in (12 x 7cm) and trim the corners with a corner punch. Glue to the white card.

6. Glue the vase and flowers to the card with glue dots.

7. Attach a lilac bow to finish.

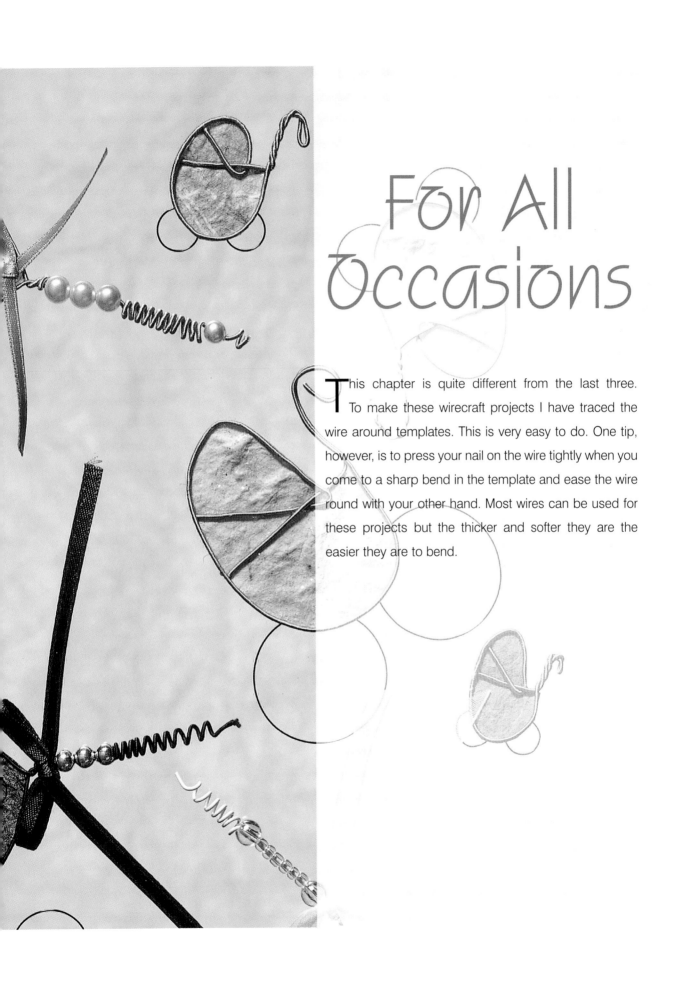

For All Occasions

This chapter is quite different from the last three. To make these wirecraft projects I have traced the wire around templates. This is very easy to do. One tip, however, is to press your nail on the wire tightly when you come to a sharp bend in the template and ease the wire round with your other hand. Most wires can be used for these projects but the thicker and softer they are the easier they are to bend.

Cream Heart

This card is made entirely of a beautiful handmade paper that has petals, leaves and grasses embedded in it. It provides a wonderful texture and makes the card look really special. I have used the same paper for the centre of the heart and added pearl beads and a pink ribbon.

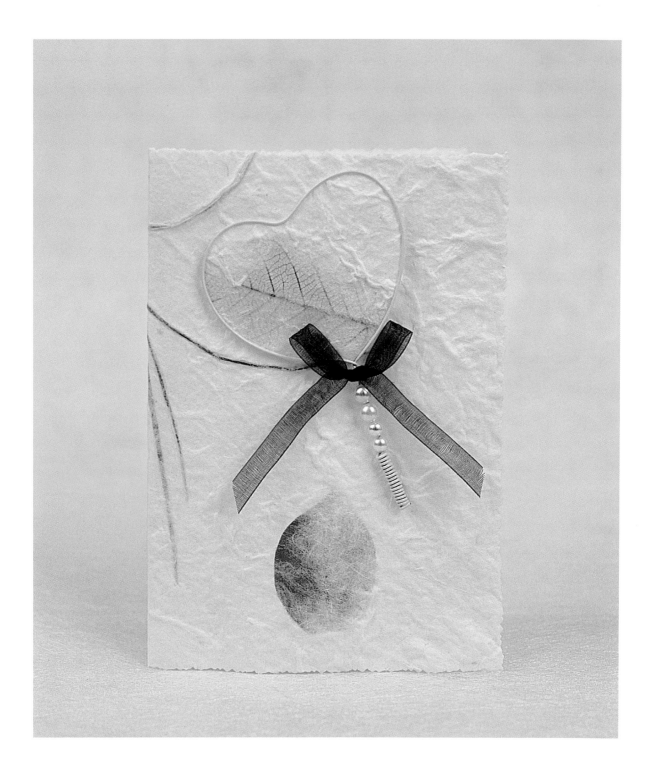

The instructions:

1. Cut 12in (30cm) of white plastic-coated wire.

2. With one end of the wire overlapping the start point (A) by ¼in (1cm), trace the wire around the large heart template below, holding the wire down every ¾–1¼in (2–3cm) as you proceed around the template until you reach the wire join point (B).

3. Pick up the heart and gently twist the wires together at point B to secure.

4. Cut off the shorter wire and thread four pearlized beads as far up the wire as possible.

You will need:

Wirecraft
12in (30cm) white
    plastic-coated wire

4 pearlized beads

Cocktail stick

Cream handmade paper

Card
8½ x 5½in (22 x 14cm) cream
    handmade paper

Foam pads

Pink ribbon

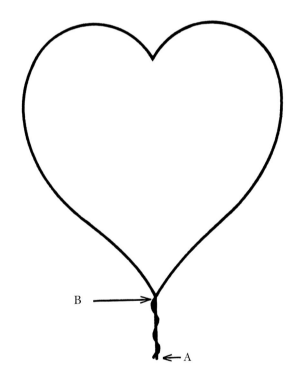

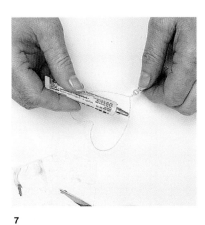

5. Wrap the tip of the wire around a cocktail stick to curl.

6. Cut a piece of handmade paper larger than the heart.

7. Turn the heart to the back and run a thin strip of glue onto the frame.

8. Quickly remove the excess glue with a paper towel. Attach the paper to the glued frame, gently squeezing between your finger and thumb.

9. Use fine scissors to trim the paper away from the frame, getting as close to the frame as possible.

7

To make the card:

1. Score and fold cream handmade paper measuring 8½ x 5½in (22 x 14cm).

2. Insert a piece of cream paper inside the card if required.

3. Attach the heart with foam pads to raise it from the card.

4. Add a pink bow.

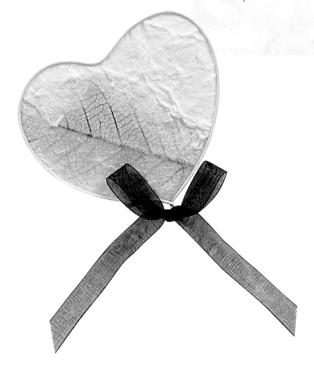

White Heart

This is a variation of the cream heart card on page 84. Here, a white heart with pretty white organza ribbon and silver beads makes this card particularly suitable for a wedding or special anniversary. The layers of paper on the card provide a pleasing three-dimensional effect.

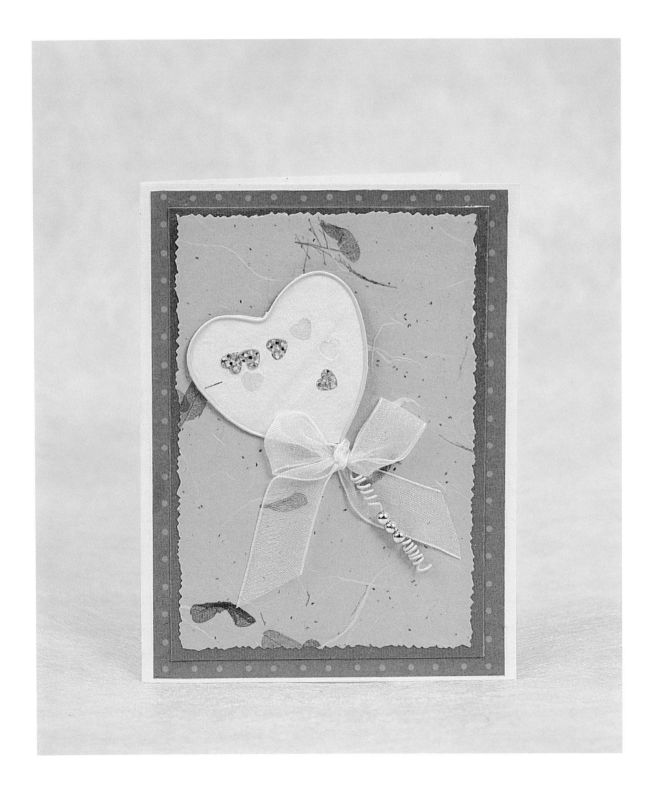

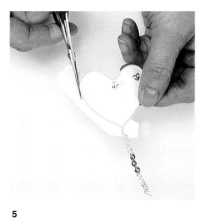

5

The instructions:

1. Cut 12in (30cm) of white plastic-coated wire.

2. Follow the template for the medium-size heart, below, and steps 1–3 on page 85.

3. Twist the end of the wire around a cocktail stick for a few turns, add three silver beads then continue to twist the wire around the stick.

4. Apply glue to the frame and attach white mulberry paper (see the Cream Heart, steps 6–9, page 86).

5. Trim the paper with fine scissors.

6. Make a white bow with organza ribbon and tie at the base of the heart.

To make the card:

1. Score and fold white card measuring 8½ x 5½in (22 x 14cm).

2. Cut and glue blue dotted paper measuring 5¼ x 4in (13.5 x 10cm).

3. Cut and glue blue pearlized card measuring 5 x 3½in (12.5 x 9cm).

4. Cut blue handmade paper measuring 4¾ x 3¼in (12 x 8.5cm). Trim with deckle-edged scissors then glue to the blue pearlized card.

5. Glue the heart to the card with a glue dot.

You will need:

Wirecraft
12in (30cm) white plastic-coated wire

Cocktail stick

3 silver beads

White mulberry paper (with silver hearts)

White organza ribbon

Card
8½ x 5½in (22 x 14cm) white card

5¼ x 4in (13.5 x 10cm) blue dotted paper

5 x 3½in (12.5 x 9cm) blue pearlized paper

4¾ x 3¼in (12 x 8.5cm) blue handmade paper

Deckle-edged scissors

Glue dot

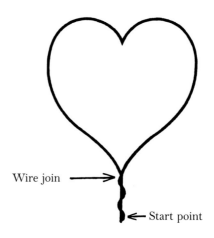

Wire join ⟶

⟵ Start point

Love Heart

The simple but effective heart design is used again here, but this time the deep red I have chosen sends a different message. This gift card is the perfect way to show someone how much you care. The time and effort that you put into making this card will say a lot.

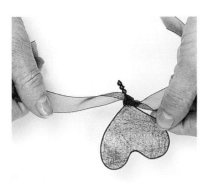

The instructions:

1. Using 12in (30cm) of red wire, follow the template for the medium-size heart on page 88 and steps 1–3 on page 85.

2. Thread three gold beads and secure the wire by bending it underneath the beads, after trimming the wire to approximately ¼in (1cm).

3. Glue red mulberry paper to the heart and trim with curved scissors (see the Cream Heart, steps 6–9, page 86).

4. Tie a red bow to hide the join at the base of the heart.

4

You will need:

Wirecraft
12in (30cm) red wire

Red mulberry paper

3 gold beads

Red ribbon

Card
8½ x 5½in (22 x 14cm) white card

5 x 3¼in (12.5 x 8.5cm) white card

5 x 3½in (13 x 9cm) red card

Heart-shaped stamp

Square shadow stamp

White ink pad

Red ink pad

Deckle-edged scissors

Glue dots

To make the card:

1. Score and fold white card measuring 8½ x 5½in (22 x 14cm).

2. Cut red card measuring 5 x 3½in (13 x 9cm) and stamp with a heart shape in white ink. Glue to centre of the white card.

3. Cut white card measuring 5 x 3¼in (12.5 x 8.5cm). Stamp with a square shadow stamp in red ink. Trim with deckle-edged scissors then glue to the card.

4. Attach the heart with glue dots.

Golden Hearts

This striking and unusual card could be used for almost any occasion and would be appreciated by both men and women. The combination of gold and turquoise gives it a really stylish and contemporary look and the gold webbing underneath the hearts provides great texture.

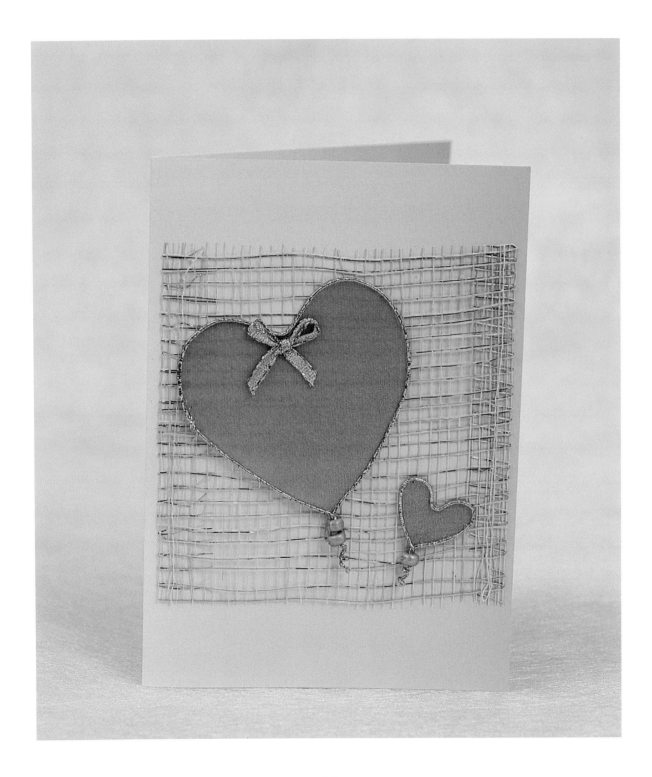

The instructions:

1. Using gold textured wire, follow the large heart template and steps 1–3 on page 85. Twist the wire at the join point.

2. Add two blue beads and wrap the end of the wire around a cocktail stick to finish.

3. Make a tiny heart following the small heart template, below, and add one blue bead.

4. Attach gold pearlized paper to both hearts (see the Cream Heart, steps 6–9, page 86).

5. Decorate with a gold bow to finish.

3

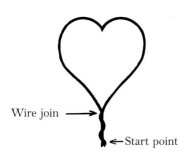

Wire join ⟶

⟵ Start point

To make the card:

1. Score and fold blue card measuring 8¼ x 6in (21 x 15cm).

2. Cut and glue a piece of gold mesh measuring 4 x 4in (10 x 10cm).

3. Attach the golden hearts with glue dots.

You will need:

Wirecraft
12in (30cm) gold textured wire

Gold pearlized paper

3 blue beads

Cocktail stick

Gold ribbon

Card
8¼ x 6in (21 x 15cm) blue card

4 x 4in (10 x 10cm) gold mesh

Glue dots

Red Hearts

This flexible design makes an ideal base for a Valentine's or anniversary card. The precise decoration can be altered to suit the recipient.

In this case, the red bow adds a degree of femininity, but without it this card would also be perfect to give to a man.

The instructions:

1. Cut a length of red wire measuring 14in (35cm). Find the centre and form a loop that is ¾in (2cm) long. Twist together three times. Form a second ¾in (2cm) loop ¼in (1cm) away from the first on the left of the wire. Form a third ¾in (2cm) loop ¼in (1cm) away from the centre on the right. Twist the two ends together and shape into a heart.

2. Shape each loop into a heart.

3. Thread five red beads and wrap the end of the wire around a cocktail stick to shape.

4. Cut and glue red mulberry paper to the back of the hearts (see the Cream Heart, steps 6–9, page 86). Trim with curved scissors.

5. Tie a bow to cover the wire join.

Tip

It is helpful to use a pencil to gently bend the wire into a heart shape. While you push the centre in with your fingers the pencil keeps the rounded sides.

You will need:

Wirecraft
14in (35cm) red wire

5 red beads

Cocktail stick

Red mulberry paper

Red ribbon

Card
8¼ x 4¼in (21 x 10.5cm) white card

4 x 4in (10 x 10cm) red card

3½ x 3½in (9 x 9cm) silver card

Decorative corner punch

Glue dot

To make the card:

1. Score and fold white card measuring 8¼ x 4¼in (21 x 10.5cm).

2. Cut and glue red card measuring 4 x 4in (10 x 10cm).

3. Cut silver card measuring 3½ x 3½in (9 x 9cm) and punch the corners before gluing to the red card.

4. Attach the hearts with a glue dot underneath the bow.

2

Pram

This simple pram design makes a very sweet card to welcome a new baby boy or girl. The border around the card is echoed by the square stamps in the centre of the card and the thick handmade paper provides a wonderful texture, giving the card an extra touch of quality.

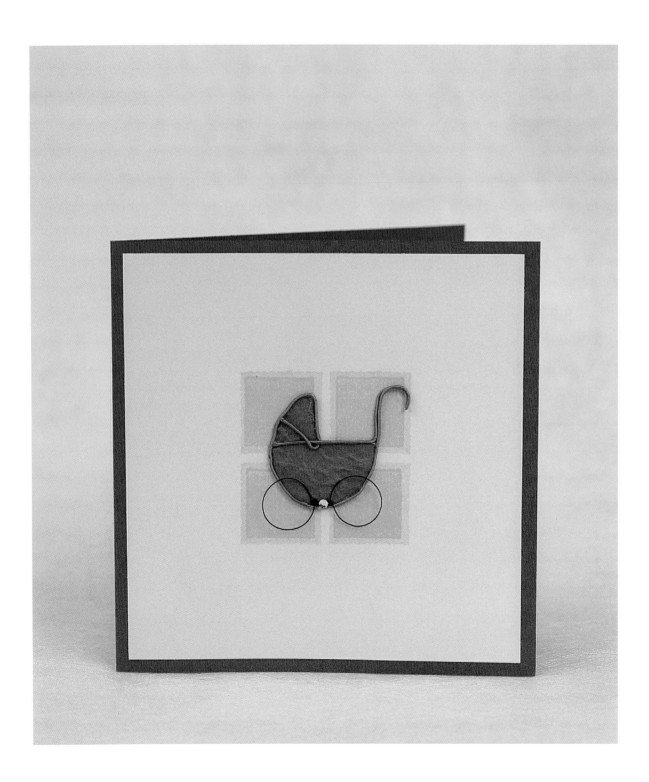

You will need:

Wirecraft
12in (30cm) purple wire

8in (20cm) 28-gauge
  dark-coloured wire

Purple mulberry paper

Thick pen or glue lid

Card
12 x 6in (30 x 15cm) purple card

5½ x 5½in (14 x 14cm) white card

Large shadow stamp

Small shadow shamp

Purple ink pad

Lilac ink pad

Glue or foam dots

Diamond dot or bow

The instructions:

1. Cut 12in (30cm) of purple wire.

2. Hold one end of the wire down with your finger at point A on the template – overlap A by ¼in (1cm). Using a second finger, hold the wire at point B and bend the wire up to form the handle (point C).

3. Bend the wire back on itself and down past point B (keeping your finger on B, bend the wire by moving your fingers along the wire as you go around the bottom of the pram).

4. Hold a finger on point A and bend the wire round. Holding your finger on the wire at points D and E, bend the wire down to point F.

5. Pick up the frame and tuck the wire from E under and over the cross wire and up to D. (Don't trim the ends of the wire now. Wait until you have covered it with paper when it will be more secure.)

6. Cut a piece of purple mulberry paper that is larger than the pram. Turn the frame over and place a very thin strip of glue on the frame. Wipe off as much of the excess glue as possible with a paper towel and quickly and gently press the paper onto the glued frame.

7. Trim away the excess paper and wire at points A and D.

8. To make the wheels, cut an 8in (20cm) length of 28-gauge dark-coloured wire. Hold the centre of the wire around a thick pen or glue lid (or anything round and larger than a pencil). Twist three times for one wheel. Twist the other side of the wire to make a second wheel. Trim off the excess wire.

9. Glue the wheels to the bottom of the pram, either on top or underneath.

9

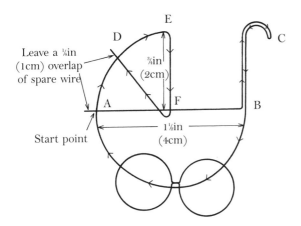

E

D

Leave a ¼in
(1cm) overlap
of spare wire

¾in
(2cm)

A   F   B

1½in
(4cm)

Start point

C

To make the card:

1. Score and fold a piece of purple card measuring 12 x 6in (30 x 15cm).

2. Cut a piece of white card measuring 5½ x 5½in (14 x 14cm).

3. Stamp four squares in purple ink, using a shadow stamp.

4. To achieve the three-dimensional effect, stamp over each square again with a small shadow stamp and lilac ink.

5. Glue the pram to centre of the card, either with glue or foam dots.

6. Add a diamond dot or a small bow to cover the wire join.

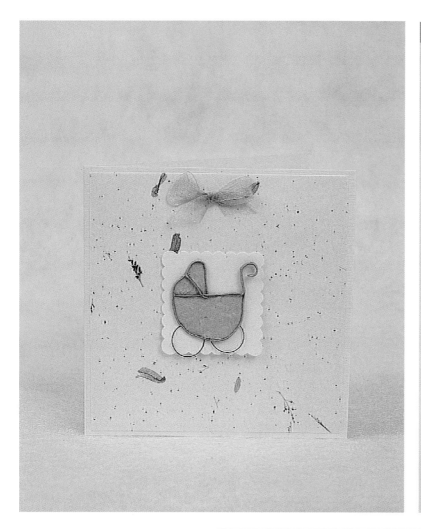

You will need:

Wirecraft

12in (30cm) pink wire

8in (20cm) 28-gauge
    dark-coloured wire

Pink mulberry paper

Thick pen or glue lid

Card

12 x 6in (30 x 15cm) white card

2¼ x 2¼in (5.5 x 5.5cm) white card

5½ x 5½in (14 x 14cm) handmade
    backing paper

Square scalloped punch or
    decorative-edged scissors

Foam pads

Glue dots

Pink organza ribbon

To make the card:

1. Score and fold in half a piece of white card measuring 12 x 6in
   (30 x 15cm).

2. Cut and glue a piece of handmade backing paper measuring 5½ x 5½in
   (14 x 14cm).

3. Punch a scalloped square measuring 2¼in (5.5cm) out of white card or
   cut a square with decorative-edged scissors. Attach it with foam pads
   so that it is raised from the card.

4. Attach the pram with glue dots.

5. Add a bow to finish.

Baby's Bib

This is another card to celebrate the arrival of a new baby. The lemon yellow and green colour combination makes it equally suitable for a boy or a girl. Of course, if you know the gender of the baby beforehand, you can make the card in colours to suit.

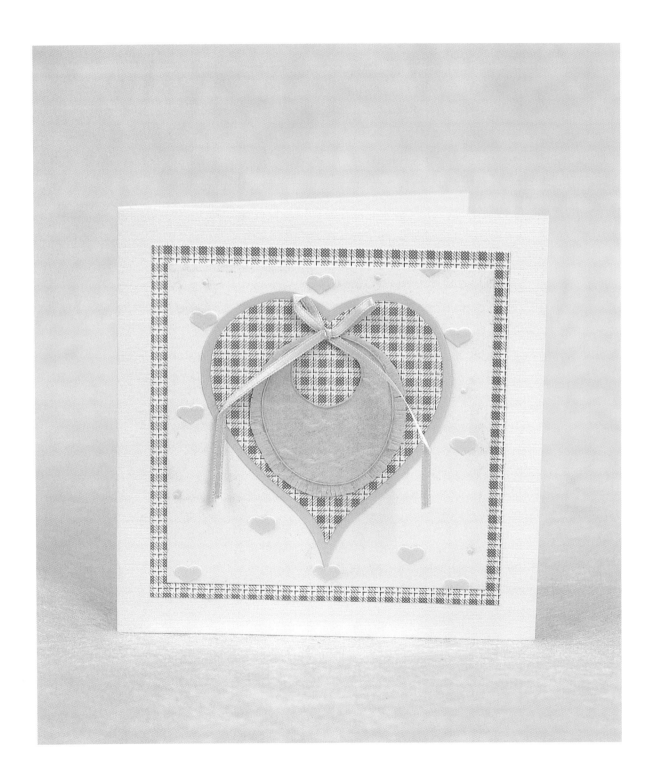

The instructions:

1. Cut a 10in (25cm) length of yellow plastic-coated wire. Place the end of the wire ¼in (1cm) over point A on the template.

2. Follow the template round, pressing the wire with your finger every ¼in (1cm) until you reach point B.

3. Make a sharp bend at point B, and then follow the bend round (holding the wire down as you bend it) to point A.

4. Do not twist the wires together where they meet, cut them off after you have added the paper, as they will stay together when the paper is attached and will be hidden by the ribbon.

5. Cut a piece of yellow handmade paper that is larger than the bib.

6. Place a very thin layer of glue over the back of the wire frame. Remove the excess with a paper towel as quickly as possible and place the paper over the glued frame, gently pressing between finger and thumb.

7. Trim the paper ⅛in (5mm) away from the wire, and then finally trim the wire from point A.

8. Snip the paper up to the wire to form a frill.

9. Add a bow for the finishing touch.

You will need:

Wirecraft
10in (25cm) length of yellow plastic-coated wire

Yellow handmade paper

Card
12 x 6in (30 x 15cm) white card

4¼ x 4¼in (11 x 11cm) white card

5 x 5in (12.5 x 12.5cm) green gingham backing paper

Approx. 4 x 4in (10 x 10cm) yellow paper

Approx. 3 x 3in (8 x 8cm) green gingham backing paper

Yellow pastel chalks

Lightbox

Embossing tool

Pale green bow

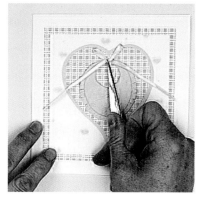

9

Baby's Bib

To make the card:

1. Score and fold white card measuring 12 x 6in (30 x 15cm).

2. Cut and glue green gingham backing paper measuring 5 x 5in
   (12.5 x 12.5cm) and glue to the white card.

3. Cut and dry emboss (see page 62 for dry embossing technique)
   hearts and dots onto a piece of white card measuring 4¼ x 4¼in
   (11 x 11cm). Colour the embossed images with yellow pastel chalks
   and glue to the gingham paper.

4. Cut a heart out of yellow paper measuring approximately 4 x 4in
   (10 x 10cm).

5. Cut a smaller heart out of green gingham paper measuring
   approximately 3 x 3in (8 x 8cm) and glue to the yellow heart.

6. Cut around the outside of the yellow heart, leaving approximately
   ⅛in (3mm) of it showing, then glue to the card.

7. Glue the bib to centre of the gingham heart and attach a green bow
   with a glue dot to hide the wire join.

Excess wire to trim
when finished

B   A

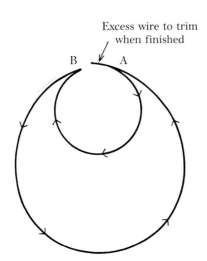

Yellow Cross

I have found that there is a lack of cards for Christian occasions, so I thought that I would design this cross. It can be used for a variety of religious occasions, depending on the colours chosen. This bright yellow design would make a particularly nice Easter card.

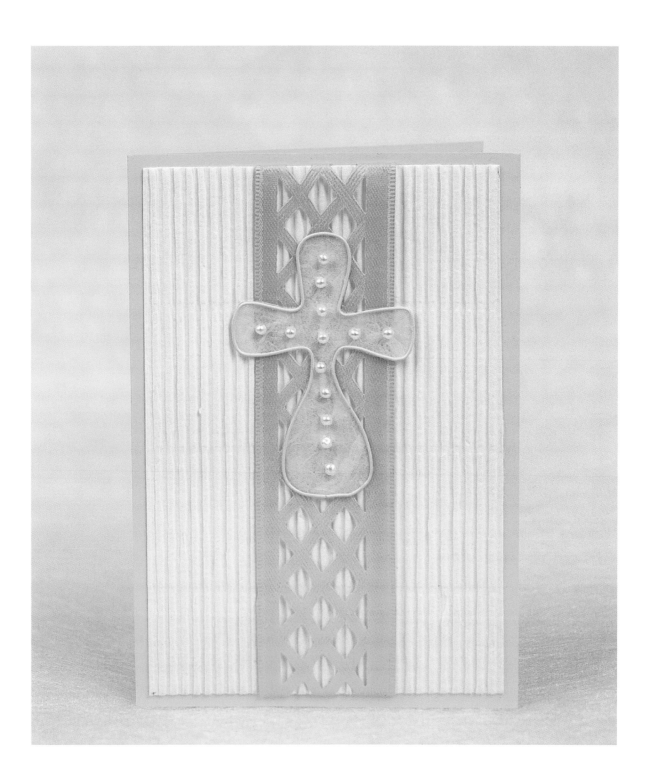

The instructions:

1. Cut 12in (30cm) of white plastic-coated wire. Hold your finger over the wire on join point A.

2. Trace the wire around the template with your fingers, holding the wire down every ¾–1¼in (2–3cm) as you proceed around the cross.

3. Cut the ends of the wire together at the join point to get a clean-cut edge.

4. Cut yellow mulberry paper a little larger than the cross.

5. Place a thin strip of glue to the back of the cross and quickly wipe the excess off with a paper towel. Attach the paper to the glued frame.

6. Trim away the excess paper as close to the frame as possible with nail/fine scissors.

7. Decorate with pearlized beads.

You will need:

Wirecraft
12in (30cm) white plastic-coated wire

Yellow mulberry paper

Approx. 13 pearlized beads

Card
8¼ x 6in (21 x 15cm) yellow card

5½ x 4in (14 x 10cm) white corrugated card

Yellow ribbon

Glue dots

To make the card:

1. Score and fold a piece of yellow card measuring 8¼ x 6in (21 x 15cm).

2. Cut a piece of white corrugated card measuring 5½ x 4in (14 x 10cm).

3. Glue some yellow ribbon to the corrugated card then glue the white card onto the yellow card.

4. Attach the cross to the centre of the yellow ribbon with glue dots.

A

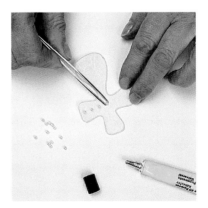

7

Silver Cross

This card is designed to give the impression of a church window, making it appropriate to send in celebration of numerous religious occasions, including baptisms, christenings and confirmations. You could alter the central cross motif to suit different religions.

You will need:

Wirecraft
12in (30cm) silver textured wire

Silver webbing ribbon

1 purple bead

Sticky tape

Card
11 x 5½in (28 x 14cm) cream card

5¼ x 5¼in (13.5 x 13.5cm) cream textured card

3¼ x 2¾in (8.5 x 7cm) cream card

Purple handmade paper

Purple mulberry paper

Scrap paper

Sponge

Purple ink pad

Glue dots

The instructions:

1. Follow the instructions for the Yellow Cross on page 102, but make the cross from silver textured wire and silver webbing ribbon.

2. Thread a piece of wire through a purple bead and push it through the centre of the cross.

3. Secure the wire at the back with a piece of tape.

3

To make the card:

1. Score and fold cream card measuring 11 x 5½in (28 x 14cm).

2. Cut cream textured card measuring 5¼ x 5¼in (13.5 x 13.5cm).

3. Cut a piece of scrap paper the shape of a window and place it on the textured card.

4. Dab over the card lightly using a sponge and a purple ink pad. Cover the scrap paper as well as the card, and when coloured sufficiently remove the scrap paper.

5. Cut a piece of purple handmade paper that is ¼in (1cm) smaller than your window shape and glue to the centre.

6. Cut a piece of cream card measuring 3¼ x 2¾in (8.5 x 7cm) and cut into the shape of a cross. Glue to the purple card.

7. Tear purple mulberry paper and glue to the cream cross.

8. Attach the cross with glue dots.

Key

This attractive silver key card with beautiful handmade paper background could be given to celebrate a new home, an 18th or 21st birthday or even to a loved one to symbolize the 'key to your heart'. You can alter the message on the background paper to suit the occasion.

The instructions:

1. Cut a length of silver textured wire measuring 10in (25cm). Starting at the wire join point (A) on the template, hold your finger down on the wire.

2. Follow the template round, holding the wire down tightly when you reach a bend or corner. When you have reached point C, twist the top of the key between points B and C then continue to the end. Don't trim the wires off at this point – just overlap them for now; they will be secured when they are glued to the paper, then they can be cut off.

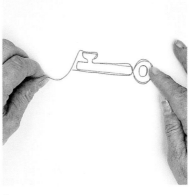

2

You will need:

Wirecraft

10in (25cm) silver textured wire

1¼in (3cm) silver-coated wire

Silver webbing ribbon

White ribbon

Card

12 x 6in (30 x 15cm) white card

5½ x 5½in (14 x 14cm) handmade backing paper

4¼ x 4¼in (11 x 11cm) silver card

4¼ x 4¼in (11 x 11cm) purple pearlized card

3½ x 3½in (9 x 9cm) greetings acetate

Lace punch

Glue dots

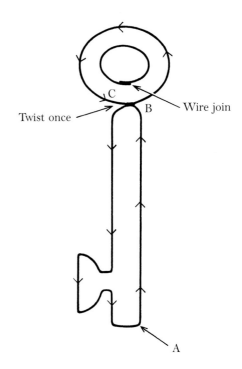

3. Cut a piece of silver webbing ribbon that is larger than the key.

4. Turn the key over and smear a thin layer of glue on the wire frame, working quickly to remove the excess with a paper towel.

5. Place the webbing ribbon on the glued frame and trim the excess with fine scissors. (Trim off the ends of the wires at this point.)

6. Cut 1¼in (3cm) of wire and make a circle. Stick this to the centre of the key to make the ring. Trim away the inner circle ribbon to leave a 'hole' close to the inside of the circle.

7. Tie a white bow at the top of the key.

To make the card:

1. Score and fold white card measuring 12 x 6in (30 x 15cm).

2. Cut and glue handmade backing paper measuring 5½ x 5½in (14 x 14cm).

3. Cut and glue silver card measuring 4¼ x 4¼in (11 x 11cm).

4. Cut purple pearlized paper measuring 4¼ x 4¼in (11 x 11cm) and use a punch to create a lace edge. Glue to the silver card.

5. Cut greetings acetate measuring 3½ x 3½in (9 x 9cm). Glue to the card, but make sure the glue is only under where you will glue the key, otherwise it will show through the acetate.

6. Attach the key with glue dots.

You will need:

Wirecraft
10in (25cm) green
   plastic-coated wire

1¼in (3cm) green
   plastic-coated wire

Green mulberry paper

Green ribbon

Card
8½ x 6in (22 x 15cm) green card

4¼ x 3in (11 x 8cm) white card

4 x 2¾in (10 x 7cm) green
   backing paper

3½ x 1¾in (9 x 4cm)
   mulberry paper

4¾ x 3½in (12 x 9cm) black card

Flower stamp

Deckle-edged scissors

To make the card:

1. Score and fold green card measuring 8½ x 6in (22 x 15cm).

2. Stamp the front of the card with a flower stamp.

3. Cut, deckle edge and glue a piece of black card measuring 4¾ x 3½in (12 x 9cm).

4. Cut and glue white card measuring 4¾ x 3in (11 x 8cm).

5. Cut, deckle edge and glue green backing paper measuring 4 x 2¾in (10 x 7cm).

6. Wet-tear (see page 44) green mulberry paper measuring 3½ x 1½in (9 x 4cm), then glue in the centre.

7. Glue the key onto the card and add a bow to cover the wire join.

Guitar

This is a great card for music-lovers. I have chosen to make a guitar but you could just as easily replace it with the intended recipient's favourite instrument by drawing a simple template and tracing it with your wire, as described throughout this chapter.

The instructions:

1. For the body, cut 6in (15cm) of 28-gauge wire. Starting at the wire join, follow template A on page 113. Snip the wires at the join point, holding them together for the time being.

2. For the neck, cut 5½in (14cm) of 28-gauge wire and follow template B on page 113. Overlap the wire join at ⅛in (5mm).

3. Cut a piece of orange mulberry paper measuring 2 x 1½in (5 x 4cm). Apply a thin layer of glue to the frame and wipe off the excess with a paper towel. Holding the 'join' together, place the body onto the centre of the paper and trim away the excess paper with thin scissors.

4. Cut a piece of plain brown mulberry paper measuring 2¼ x ¼in (6 x 1cm). Place a thin layer of glue onto the wire frame as before, attach to the wire neck, and trim the excess paper. Add an orange piece of paper for the headstock.

You will need:

Wirecraft

6in (15cm) 28-gauge wire

5½in (14cm) 28-gauge wire

2 x 1½in (5 x 4cm) orange mulberry paper

2¼ x ¼in (6 x 1cm) brown mulberry paper

Black felt-tipped pen/black biro

Card

12 x 6in (30 x 15cm) white card

4¼ x 4¼in (11 x 11cm) orange card

4 x 4in (10.5 x 10.5cm) music backing paper

3¾ x 2in (9.5 x 5cm) orange card

3½ x 1½in (9 x 4cm) white card

Double-sided tape

3 white beads

4 musical note motifs

Tip

Before using your felt-tipped pen, test it on a spare peice of mulberry paper. Some felt-tips bleed when used on this paper so you may need to use a black biro or similar pen.

7

5. Place the base over template A and then with a black felt-tipped pen draw the sound hole and the bridge.

6. Draw the frets and inlays on the neck with the felt-tipped pen and the thin strips in the headstock (see Tip on page 111).

7. Glue the neck to the base at the sound hole. Don't glue on the beads for the tuning pegs yet – wait until the guitar is attached to the card.

To make the card:

1. Score and fold a piece of white card measuring 12 x 6in (30 x 15cm).

2. Cut and glue orange card measuring 4¼ x 4¼in (11 x 11cm).

3. Cut and glue music backing paper measuring 4 x 4in (10.5 x 10.5cm).

4. Cut and glue orange card measuring 3¾ x 2in (9.5 x 5cm).

5. Cut and glue white card measuring 3½ x 1½in (9 x 4cm).

6. Attach the guitar with double-sided tape then glue three white beads on either side of the headstock.

7. Attach musical notes to the four corners of the card.

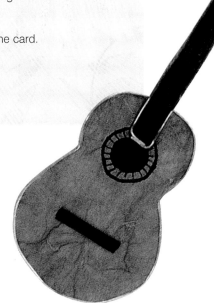

Template A

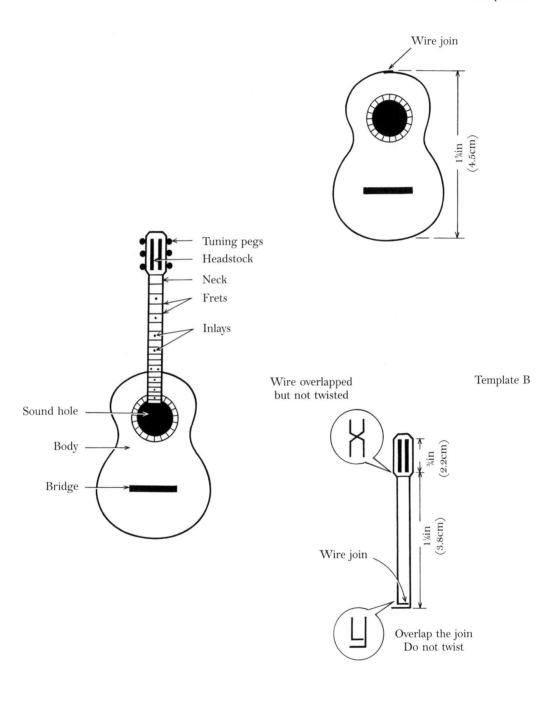

Wire join

1¾in
(4.5cm)

Tuning pegs

Headstock

Neck

Frets

Inlays

Sound hole

Body

Bridge

Wire overlapped
but not twisted

Template B

⅞in
(2.2cm)

1½in
(3.8cm)

Wire join

Overlap the join
Do not twist

Sailing Boat

This stylish card has a great tactile quality to it due to the effect of the wet-torn mulberry paper, which looks almost like feathers. This effective technique could be used with a variety of designs. Here it has been combined with a boat motif, making it an ideal birthday or Father's Day card.

The instructions:

1. For the base of the boat, cut 6in (15cm) of blue wire. Overlap point A by ¼in (1cm), then follow the arrows round the template (see page 116). At each point or turn, hold your finger down on the wire while you bend it. When you reach point A again, trim off the wire (they will stay together when you add the paper).

2. For the sails, cut 12in (30cm) of blue wire. Starting at point A, follow the arrows up to point B. Hold your finger on the wire as you turn the corner, then continue round the sails until you reach point B again. Place the end of wire in the bend at point B then trim off.

3. Cut two pieces of blue mulberry paper that are larger than the wire frame requires.

4. Turn the boat over and place a very thin layer of glue along the frame. Remove the excess glue as quickly as possible with a paper towel.

5. Place the mulberry paper onto the glued frame, gently holding them together with your fingers and thumbs.

6. Turn the boat the right way up and trim away the excess paper with fine scissors.

6

You will need:

Wirecraft
6in (15cm) blue wire

12in (30cm) blue wire

Blue mulberry paper

Card
8½ x 8¼in (22 x 21cm) blue card

8 x 4in (20 x 10cm) silver card

7 x 3½in (18 x 9cm) boat-motif backing paper

4¾ x 3in (12 x 8cm) blue mulberry paper

4 x 2½in (10 x 6.5cm) silver card

3¾ x 2¼in (9.5 x 6cm) blue corrugated card

3½ x 2in (9 x 5cm) silver card

3¼ x 1¾in (8.5 x 4.5cm) orange mulberry paper

Foam pads

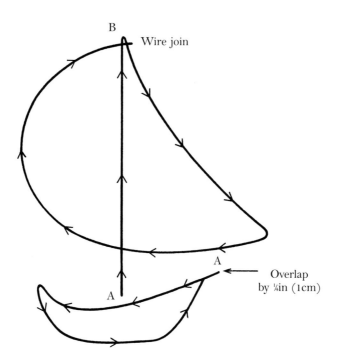

B

Wire join

A

A

Overlap
by ⅜in (1cm)

To make the card:

1. Score and fold blue card measuring 8½ x 8¼in (22 x 21cm).

2. Cut and glue silver card measuring 8 x 4in (20 x 10cm).

3. Cut, deckle edge and glue a piece of boat backing paper measuring 7 x 3½in (18 x 9cm).

4. Wet-tear (see page 44) blue mulberry paper measuring 4¾ x 3in (12 x 8cm) then glue it to the boat paper.

5. Cut and glue silver card measuring 4 x 2½in (10 x 6.5cm).

6. Cut and glue blue corrugated card measuring 3¾ x 2¼in (9.5 x 6cm).

7. Cut, deckle edge and glue silver card measuring 3½ x 2in (9 x 5cm).

8. Wet-tear orange mulberry paper measuring 3¼ x 1¾in (8.5 x 4.5cm) and glue to the silver card.

9. Glue the boat with foam pads.

Christmas Bell

This special Christmas card has plenty of festive sparkle and is sure to be loved by all who receive it. As an alternative, the holly could be replaced with bride and groom figures and the bell could be made in different colours to represent a wedding bell!

The instructions:

1. Cut 12in (30cm) of silver textured wire. Holding the wire at point A, follow the template round the side of the bell to point B.

2. Form a circle with a ¼in (1cm) diameter and twist the wire twice to form a ring.

3. Continue down the other side of the bell back to point A again.

4. Thread the two wires through a silver bead and wrap each one round a cocktail stick to twist; this will also secure the bell shape. Trim the ends.

5. Turn the bell over and place a thin layer of glue onto the wire frame. Remove the excess with a paper towel.

6. Cut a 2¾in (7cm) square piece of red mulberry paper and place gently on the wire frame holding them together with your fingers and thumb.

7. Trim the excess paper close to the wire with a pair of fine scissors.

8. Glue a row of beads to the bell for decoration then attach a silver bow.

You will need:

Wirecraft
12in (30cm) silver textured wire

1 silver bead

Cocktail stick

2¾in (7cm) square red mulberry paper

Approx. 17 small silver beads

Silver ribbon

Card
8½ x 8¼in (22 x 21cm) red card

8 x 3½in (20 x 9cm) silver card

6 x 3¼in (15 x 8cm) cream card

Christmas greeting stamp

Green ink pad

Glue dots

8

To make the card:

1. Score and fold red card measuring 8½ x 8¼in (22 x 21cm).

2. Cut and glue silver card measuring 8 x 3½in (20 x 9cm).

3. Cut and glue cream card stamped with a Christmas greeting in green ink.

4. Attach the bell with glue dots.

5. To finish, make and attach the wire holly, following the instructions on page 44.

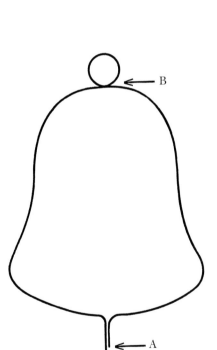

Mail Order Craft Suppliers

Australia

Australia Craft Network
PO Box 350
Narellan
NSW 2567
Tel: +61 (02) 4647 7047
Fax: +61 (02) 8572 8256
www.auscraftnet.com

Canada

So-Facile Canada Inc
9320 Boul St Laurent
Suite 405
Montral
Quebec
Canada
H2N-1N7
Tel: +1 514 382 3090
Fax: +1 514 382 3688
www.so-facile.com

New Zealand

Scrapbook Alley
Shop 5
17 Trinity Crescent
Napier
NZ
Tel: +64 842 2317
www.scrapbookalley.co.nz

UK

Artycrafty
9 Church Street
Godalming
Surrey
GU7 1EQ
Tel: +44 (0)1483 427133
www.artycrafty.com
e-mail: artycrafty@aol.com

Craft Crazy
2 Barley Road
Thelwall
Warrington
Cheshire
WA4 2EZ
Tel: +44 (0)1925 263263
www.craftcrazy.co.uk

Craft Creations Ltd.
4B Ingersol House
Delamare Road
Cheshunt
Hertfordshire
EN8 9HD
Tel: +44 (0)1992 781900
www.craftcreations.com

CraftDee
43/44 Market H:all
Arndale Centre
Luton
Bedfordshire
LU1 2TA
Tel: +44 (0)1582 414043
www.craftdee.co.uk

Fred Aldous (CB01)
37 Lever Street
Manchester
M1 1LW
Tel: +44 (0)8707 517301/2

Hobbicraft
Dept. CB
40 Woodhouse Lane
Merrion Centre
Leeds
LS2 8LX
www.hobbicraft.co.uk

Hobbycraft
The Arts and Crafts Superstore
www.hobbycraft.co.uk
Freephone: +44 (0)800 027 2387

Impress Cards and Craft Materials
Dept. CB
Slough Farm
Westhall
Halesworth
Suffolk
IP19 8RN
Tel: +44 (0)1986 781422
www.impresscards.com

Kelridge Craft Pals (CB)
23 Lockley Street
Northwood
Stoke-on-Trent
Staffordshire
ST1 6PQ
www.kelridge-craft-pals.co.uk

Lakeland Limited
Alexandra Buildings
Windermere
Cumbria
LA23 1BQ
Tel: +44 (0)1539 488100
www.lakelandlimited.co.uk

Rogate Paper Supplies
Bowness Avenue
Sompting
Lancing
West Sussex
BN15 9TP
Tel: +44 (0)1903 755208
www.rogatepaper.co.uk

The Craft Barn
9 East Grinstead Road
Lingfield
Surrey
RH7 6EP
Tel: +44 (0)1342 836097
www.craftbarn.co.uk

Topaz Crafts (CB)
Oswaldtwistle Mills
Colliers Street
Oswaldtwistle
Accrington
Lancashire
BB5 3DE
Tel: +44 (0)1254 770702/3
www.topazcrafts.co.uk

USA
Crafts, etc!
7717 SW 44th Street
Oklahoma City
Ok 73179
(Domestic) Tel: +1 806 888 0321
(International) Tel: +1 405 745 1200
www.craftsetc.com

About the Author

Kate MacFadyen has always enjoyed crafts and is a highly qualified guide to the subject. Her hobbies include painting, cross stitch, making dolls' houses, plus the odd spot of gardening. She indulges in her love of all things creative by working at a craft shop, where she also teaches card-making and wirecraft.

Index

GMC Publications

BOOKS

WOODCARVING

Beginning Woodcarving	*GMC Publications*
Carving Architectural Detail in Wood: The Classical Tradition	
	Frederick Wilbur
Carving Birds & Beasts	*GMC Publications*
Carving Classical Styles in Wood	*Frederick Wilbur*
Carving the Human Figure: Studies in Wood and Stone	*Dick Onians*
Carving Nature: Wildlife Studies in Wood	*Frank Fox-Wilson*
Celtic Carved Lovespoons: 30 Patterns	*Sharon Littley & Clive Griffin*
Decorative Woodcarving (New Edition)	*Jeremy Williams*
Elements of Woodcarving	*Chris Pye*
Figure Carving in Wood: Human and Animal Forms	*Sara Wilkinson*
Lettercarving in Wood: A Practical Course	*Chris Pye*
Relief Carving in Wood: A Practical Introduction	*Chris Pye*
Woodcarving for Beginners	*GMC Publications*
Woodcarving Made Easy	*Cynthia Rogers*
Woodcarving Tools, Materials & Equipment (New Edition in 2 vols.)	
	Chris Pye

WOODTURNING

Bowl Turning Techniques Masterclass	*Tony Boase*
Chris Child's Projects for Woodturners	*Chris Child*
Decorating Turned Wood: The Maker's Eye	*Liz & Michael O'Donnell*
Green Woodwork	*Mike Abbott*
A Guide to Work-Holding on the Lathe	*Fred Holder*
Keith Rowley's Woodturning Projects	*Keith Rowley*
Making Screw Threads in Wood	*Fred Holder*
Segmented Turning: A Complete Guide	*Ron Hampton*
Turned Boxes: 50 Designs	*Chris Stott*
Turning Green Wood	*Michael O'Donnell*
Turning Pens and Pencils	*Kip Christensen & Rex Burningham*
Wood for Woodturners	*Mark Baker*
Woodturning: Forms and Materials	*John Hunnex*
Woodturning: A Foundation Course (New Edition)	*Keith Rowley*
Woodturning: A Fresh Approach	*Robert Chapman*
Woodturning: An Individual Approach	*Dave Regester*
Woodturning: A Source Book of Shapes	*John Hunnex*
Woodturning Masterclass	*Tony Boase*
Woodturning Projects: A Workshop Guide to Shapes	*Mark Baker*

WOODWORKING

Beginning Picture Marquetry	*Lawrence Threadgold*
Carcass Furniture	*GMC Publications*
Celtic Carved Lovespoons: 30 Patterns	*Sharon Littley & Clive Griffin*
Celtic Woodcraft	*Glenda Bennett*
Celtic Woodworking Projects	*Glenda Bennett*
Complete Woodfinishing (Revised Edition)	*Ian Hosker*
David Charlesworth's Furniture-Making Techniques	*David Charlesworth*
David Charlesworth's Furniture-Making Techniques – Volume 2	
	David Charlesworth
Furniture Projects with the Router	*Kevin Ley*

Furniture Restoration (Practical Crafts)	*Kevin Jan Bonner*
Furniture Restoration: A Professional at Work	*John Lloyd*
Furniture Workshop	*Kevin Ley*
Green Woodwork	*Mike Abbott*
History of Furniture: Ancient to 1900	*Michael Huntley*
Intarsia: 30 Patterns for the Scrollsaw	*John Everett*
Making Heirloom Boxes	*Peter Lloyd*
Making Screw Threads in Wood	*Fred Holder*
Making Woodwork Aids and Devices	*Robert Wearing*
Mastering the Router	*Ron Fox*
Pine Furniture Projects for the Home	*Dave Mackenzie*
Router Magic: Jigs, Fixtures and Tricks to Unleash your Router's Full Potential	*Bill Hylton*
Router Projects for the Home	*GMC Publications*
Router Tips & Techniques	*Robert Wearing*
Routing: A Workshop Handbook	*Anthony Bailey*
Routing for Beginners (Revised and Expanded Edition)	*Anthony Bailey*
Stickmaking: A Complete Course	*Andrew Jones & Clive George*
Stickmaking Handbook	*Andrew Jones & Clive George*
Storage Projects for the Router	*GMC Publications*
Success with Sharpening	*Ralph Laughton*
Veneering: A Complete Course	*Ian Hosker*
Veneering Handbook	*Ian Hosker*
Wood: Identification & Use	*Terry Porter*
Woodworking Techniques and Projects	*Anthony Bailey*
Woodworking with the Router: Professional Router Techniques any Woodworker can Use	*Bill Hylton & Fred Matlack*

UPHOLSTERY

Upholstery: A Beginners' Guide	*David James*
Upholstery: A Complete Course (Revised Edition)	*David James*
Upholstery Restoration	*David James*
Upholstery Techniques & Projects	*David James*
Upholstery Tips and Hints	*David James*

DOLLS' HOUSES AND MINIATURES

1/12 Scale Character Figures for the Dolls' House	*James Carrington*
Americana in 1/12 Scale: 50 Authentic Projects	
	Joanne Ogreenc & Mary Lou Santovec
The Authentic Georgian Dolls' House	*Brian Long*
A Beginners' Guide to the Dolls' House Hobby	*Jean Nisbet*
Celtic, Medieval and Tudor Wall Hangings in 1/12 Scale Needlepoint	
	Sandra Whitehead
Creating Decorative Fabrics: Projects in 1/12 Scale	*Janet Storey*
Dolls' House Accessories, Fixtures and Fittings	*Andrea Barham*
Dolls' House Furniture: Easy-to-Make Projects in 1/12 Scale	*Freida Gray*
Dolls' House Makeovers	*Jean Nisbett*
Dolls' House Window Treatments	*Eve Harwood*
Edwardian-Style Hand-Knitted Fashion for 1/12 Scale Dolls	
	Yvonne Wakefield

CRAFTS

GARDENING

PHOTOGRAPHY

ART TECHNIQUES

VIDEOS

MAGAZINES

WOODTURNING ◆ WOODCARVING ◆ FURNITURE & CABINETMAKING
THE ROUTER ◆ NEW WOODWORKING ◆ THE DOLLS' HOUSE MAGAZINE
OUTDOOR PHOTOGRAPHY ◆ BLACK & WHITE PHOTOGRAPHY
KNITTING ◆ GUILD NEWS

The above represents a full list of all titles currently published or scheduled to be published.
All are available direct from the Publishers or through bookshops, newsagents and specialist retailers.
To place an order, or to obtain a complete catalogue, contact:

GMC Publications,
Castle Place, 166 High Street, Lewes, East Sussex BN7 1XU United Kingdom
Tel: 01273 488005 Fax: 01273 402866
E-mail: pubs@thegmcgroup.com   Website: www.gmcbooks.com

Orders by credit card are accepted